From Mountain to Mountain

From Mountain to Mountain
Stories about Bahá'u'lláh

by
Hitjo Garst

Translated by
Olive McKinley

Illustrated by
Brian Parsons

'. . . in that day, in which they shall come to you from Assyria to Egypt, and from Egypt to the River, and from sea to sea and from mountain to mountain.'   Micah 7:12

GEORGE RONALD
OXFORD

GEORGE RONALD Publisher

Original Dutch-language edition
Von Berg tot Berg first published in 1983 by the Child Education Committee
of the National Spiritual Assembly of the Bahá'ís of the Netherlands

This translation © George Ronald 1987
Illustrations © Brian Parsons

Illustrated by Brian Parsons

British Library Cataloguing in Publication Data

Garst, Hitjo
    From mountain to mountain : stories about
    Baha'u'llah.
    1. Baha Ullah——Biography   2. Bahai Faith
    ——Biography
    I. Title
    297'.8963'0924   BP392

ISBN 0-85398-265-1 (cased)
ISBN 0-85398-266-X (paper)

Contents

Thank you
Yvonne, Esther, Yvonne, Sander, Stefan
Ineke, and Henk.
Without you this book would not have been written.

1

A New Day is Coming

Some days are special: more exciting and more wonderful than other days. When they are coming, you long and long for them to arrive, and then they pass by very quickly and are over almost before you know it.

But there is another kind of 'day', one which lasts a very long time. Do you remember the story in the Bible of how God created the world in six days? Those six days were much more than six days of a week. They were ages which lasted thousands and thousands of years. When a 'day' is mentioned in the Holy Books of God, it generally means a very long time.

The people of the world have for thousands of years been waiting for a special Day to come. The Holy Books brought by the Messengers of God to mankind have all promised that a special Day will dawn on earth – a day of peace, of tranquillity, of justice and fellowship; a day when the Word of God will take root in the hearts of all people and this world will reflect the happiness of the Kingdom of Heaven.

On that Day, just as the sun shines on the earth, there will be a wonderful Sun which shines from the Kingdom of God on all of us. We can see the physical sun with our eyes, but we must use our hearts and our minds to see the other Sun, for this is the Messenger of God Who comes on earth, and it takes a pure heart and pure eyes to see Him.

Over one hundred years ago, not just one but *two* great Messengers of God came into this world: the Báb, which means the Gate, and Bahá'u'lláh, the Glory of God. They announced the coming of that special Day promised by Isaiah, by Jesus Christ, by Buddha, Muḥammad and all the Prophets of the past. The Báb and Bahá'u'lláh sacrificed Their lives so that people on earth might find peace and happiness, so that this world might become transformed and united.

We are the lucky people who live in this age of transformation when, it is promised, the world will at last find peace.

2

The Childhood and Youth of the Báb and Bahá'u'lláh

When the Báb was a little boy He had to go to school just like other children. But one day the schoolmaster brought the young Báb home to His uncle, with whom He lived. 'I'm bringing Him back to you,' said the master. 'You must take good care of Him. He should not be treated like an ordinary child.' The master told the Báb's uncle that the boy had explained part of the Qur'án to him. It was such a wonderful explanation that the teacher was amazed. 'Keep the boy at home with you. I am not worthy to teach Him. He does not need a teacher like me,' he said.

Uncle Ḥájí Mírzá Siyyid 'Alí told the young Báb that He must go back to school and listen well to what He was taught. So the Báb returned to school; yet again and again the teacher could see that He possessed super-human wisdom. Finally His uncle decided that he would not send Him to school any more. He was just too clever to learn anything there. Instead, the Báb went to work with His uncle. He became known for His greatness and power, for the purity of His character and His extreme devotion to God.

When the Báb was twenty-four years of age, He revealed that He was the Promised One – the Qá'im – whom all the people of Persia were awaiting with eager longing. He raised the call of a new Day and foretold the coming of Bahá'u'lláh.

The Báb and Bahá'u'lláh were close in age, but They never met. The Báb was two years younger than Bahá'u'-lláh. When Bahá'u'lláh was very young, He too possessed unusual gifts. From childhood He was extremely kind and generous. He was a great lover of outdoor life, most of His time being spent in the garden or the fields. He had an extraordinary power of attraction, which was felt by all. People always crowded round Him, Ministers and people of the Court would surround Him, and the children also were devoted to Him. When He was only thirteen or fourteen He became renowned for His learning. He would converse on any subject and solve any problem presented to Him.

When Bahá'u'lláh was still a child, His father had a dream about Him. In this dream he saw Bahá'u'lláh swimming in a huge, boundless ocean. His body radiated so much light that the whole sea was illumined by it. His hair was long and dark and as He swam it flowed out about Him on the surface of the water. Then a large shoal of fish appeared and each one took the end of one hair of His head in its mouth. His face was so radiant that the fish followed Him whichever way He swam. There were a great many fish but no matter how hard they pulled at His hair, not one hair became detached. So many fish could not harm Him and neither could they prevent Him from swimming onwards.

Bahá'u'lláh's father was deeply impressed by this dream. He sent for a soothsayer and asked him to explain the dream. The soothsayer said that the sea represented the world. 'Alone and without aid, your Son will dominate the world. No one will be able to hinder His progress. All those fish represent the upheaval which He

4

will cause among the peoples of the world. They will gather round Him and attach themselves to Him. He will be protected by the Almighty and will therefore always be safe, whatever happens to Him,' he said.

Bahá'u'lláh was twenty-two years old when His father died. The Government wished Him to succeed to His father's position in the Ministry, as was customary in Iran, but Bahá'u'lláh did not accept the offer. Then the Prime Minister said: 'Leave him to himself. Such a position is unworthy of him. He has some higher aim in view. I cannot understand him, but I am convinced that he is destined for some lofty career. His thoughts are not like ours. Let him alone.'

As it was with the Báb and Bahá'u'lláh, so it has been with all the Messengers of God. They do not have to go to school to learn all the things that we have to learn. Their knowledge comes from God. They do not need to learn anything from people; people must learn from Them. They are the great Educators of mankind.

3

The Báb

When it is still winter and so cold that nothing at all can grow, the farmers work to prepare the soil. They spread manure, and plough and harrow to make the ground nice and smooth. When spring comes and the sun once more gives enough heat, the seeds and the potatoes will be sown. And this can be done because the farmers have prepared the ground beforehand.

This is what happens when a new era begins. God first sends a herald to tell people the good news: soon a new Messenger of God will come! The herald prepares the people for His coming. He helps them to believe in Him when He appears. This is what happened when Jesus came to earth. God first sent John the Baptist. He told people that Someone would come after him who was much greater than himself.

This is also what happened when God gave Bahá'u'lláh to the world. First the Báb appeared. The Báb told the people that very soon after Him Someone would come Who was much greater than Himself. He was the Promised One foretold in all the holy books, Who would bring peace on earth and Who would unite all the peoples of the world.

The first one to believe in the Báb was a lion-hearted young man named Mullá Ḥusayn. Mullá Ḥusayn knew that the time was near for the Báb to appear. He knew that only by searching very earnestly would he find Him. But he felt confident that God would lead him to the Báb, and this indeed is what happened. After praying and fasting, Mullá Ḥusayn set out. He felt his heart attracted as if by a magnet to the city of S̲h̲íráz. He reached there, and as he was walking outside the gates of the city a Youth with a shining face suddenly approached him. The Youth greeted Mullá Ḥusayn very warmly, like a friend He had known for years, and invited him to come to His home. Mullá Ḥusayn agreed and accompanied Him there.

In the course of the evening which followed, the Báb declared that He was the Qá'im, the Gate to the Promised One, and Mullá Ḥusayn became the first to believe in Him. Mullá Ḥusayn had discovered the Object of his search and found his heart's desire. He felt as if all the joys of paradise were his. That night has gone down in history.

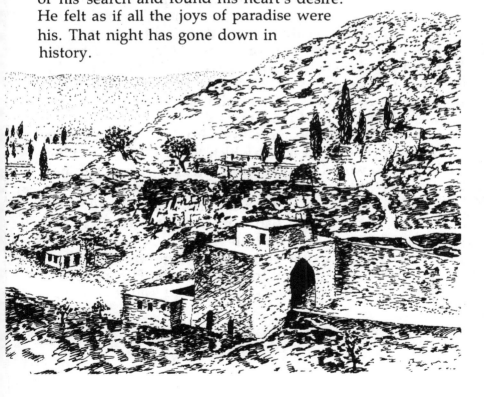

4

The Secret of Ṭihrán

Not long after the Báb had declared His mission, He asked Mullá Ḥusayn to undertake a special task for Him. He asked him to take a special Tablet, a letter which He had revealed, to Ṭihrán. He told Mullá Ḥusayn that in that city a Mystery was hidden. Mullá Ḥusayn had to discover that Mystery and see that the Báb's Tablet was delivered to Him.

So Mullá Ḥusayn set out on another journey, this time to Ṭihrán. On his way he passed through various towns and told the people living there that God had sent a new Prophet. But hardly anyone was willing to accept the new Faith. When Mullá Ḥusayn reached Ṭihrán he took a room at a boarding-school. He told the head of the school his great news. But the man did not want to listen. He was even rude to Mullá Ḥusayn.

So now Mullá Ḥusayn was in Ṭihrán. How was he to discover that secret about which the Báb had told him? To whom would he give the Tablet which the Báb had revealed? Who would know? . . . Mullá Ḥusayn had no idea. But of one thing he was certain. God would help him to carry out the Báb's orders. After all, God had already helped him to find the Báb.

Once, in the middle of the night, there was a knock on his door. It was a pupil from the school. His name was Mullá Muḥammad. Mullá Muḥammad said that he had heard how rude his teacher had been to Mullá Ḥusayn. This made Mullá Muḥammad sad. He was ashamed of his teacher.

Then Mullá Ḥusayn began asking the pupil all kinds of questions. 'What is your name? Where do you live?' He lived in Núr, in the province of Mázindarán. Then he asked if anyone belonging to the family of the famous Mírzá Buzurg of Núr had as noble a character as Mírzá Buzurg. Mullá Muḥammad said that one of the sons of Mírzá Buzurg had just as noble a character as His father.

'What is His profession?' asked Mullá Ḥusayn.

'He comforts the sorrowful and feeds the hungry.'

'What is His position?'

'He has no position except that He helps and protects the poor and the stranger.'

'And what is His name?'

'Ḥusayn-'Alí.'

Mullá Ḥusayn continued his questions. 'How does He spend His time?'

'He wanders through the woods and enjoys the beauty of the plains.'

'How old is He?'

'Twenty-eight.'

'I suppose you see Him often?'

'I frequently visit His house,' replied the pupil.

Then Mullá Ḥusayn asked the pupil if he would take something to Ḥusayn-'Alí. Mullá Muḥammad agreed. He was then given the Tablet from the Báb, rolled in a cloth. Mullá Ḥusayn asked him to take it the very next morning. And when he came back he was to come to him as quickly as possible and tell him what Mírzá Ḥusayn-'Alí had said.

As soon as it was getting light, Mullá Muḥammad

went to the house of Mírzá Ḥusayn-'Alí. There he saw one of Mírzá Ḥusayn-'Alí's brothers and told him why he had come. A moment later he was invited to come in. Mírzá Ḥusayn-'Alí unrolled the Tablet and began to read it aloud. What a splendid voice He had and how beautifully He read! Mullá Muḥammad loved listening to Him. When Mírzá Ḥusayn-'Alí had read one page He knew: these words came from God, just like the words of the Qur'án.

What do you think? Who was Mírzá Ḥusayn-'Alí? He had read only one page of the Báb's writings and He already knew that the Báb was a Messenger of God. Who else could He be but Bahá'u'lláh?

How happy Mullá Ḥusayn was when the pupil returned to him. Bahá'u'lláh had sent a gift for Mullá Ḥusayn with him: a package of tea and sugar. We would think that a very ordinary present but in those days it was very special. Mullá Ḥusayn was so glad when he received this gift that he took it in his hands and kissed it. He hugged Mullá Muḥammad and kissed his eyes.

Mullá Ḥusayn had reached his goal. He had discovered the Secret about which the Báb had spoken. Now he could travel on and tell more and more people that the Báb had appeared.

5

The King's Messenger

When the Báb began telling people that a new Messenger of God would soon come He was still quite young, just twenty-four years of age. But His words had divine power. And so it was not long before the whole of Persia knew about Him. Even the Sháh heard of Him. He wanted to know more about the Báb. And so he sent his most learned servant, Vahíd, to find out all he could about the Báb.

On the way, Vahíd thought up the questions he would ask the Báb. They were the most difficult questions he could find. Vahíd had never discovered anyone who could answer these questions. Would the Báb be able to do so?

The Báb listened attentively to Vahíd's questions. How surprised Vahíd was when the Báb then began to answer the difficult and complicated questions. These were the right answers. Vahíd was sure of that. He also knew that he himself would never have been able to find them. And he thought, too, that he was the most learned man in the land.

Vahíd wanted to ask some more questions. He went to see the Báb a second time. But when he wanted to begin, he had completely forgotten what he wanted to ask. This had never happened to him before. A few moments later he heard the Báb begin to speak. To his amazement, the

Báb was giving the answers to the questions which Vahíd had forgotten. Although Vahíd had said nothing, the Báb knew exactly what he had been going to ask.

When Vahíd went to see the Báb for the third time he had a plan. He wanted the Báb to explain a chapter from the Qur'án for him. But he would not say which chapter. If the Báb were to explain that particular chapter and do it better than he had ever heard it done, Vahíd would be certain that the Báb was a Messenger of God. Then he would become His follower.

But what happened? When Vahíd met the Báb, his whole body began to tremble. He could hardly stand on his feet. Quickly, the Báb went to him, took him by the hand and sat him down beside Him. The Báb asked what he could do for him. But Vahíd could not speak a word.

Then the Báb asked if He should explain the Suríh of Kawthar for him. Tears streamed down Vahíd's cheeks. This was exactly the chapter from the Qur'án that he had wanted the Báb to explain without being asked. When He had explained the chapter from the Qur'án, Vahíd knew for certain that the Báb had a divine Message. No one in the whole world could make him doubt this now. Vahíd then became one of the staunchest followers of the Báb.

6

Everyone Should Know

The Báb had told His first disciples quite clearly that they were to travel all over the country to make His Faith known. They must tell the people that the Promised One had now appeared. He said: 'Ye are even as the fire which in the darkness of the night has been kindled upon the mountain-top. Let your light shine before the eyes of men.' Everyone should be told that God had sent a new Messenger. After all, what is more important than the coming of a new Messenger from God?

The Báb had only a few years in which to prepare the people for the new Day. In a short time He was taken to a prison as far away as possible from His followers. His enemies thought that He would be forgotten. But that did not happen. Instead, even more people began to believe in Him.

Six years after the Báb had declared His mission to Mullá Husayn He was shot and killed by a regiment of seven hundred and fifty soldiers. At that time He was only thirty years old. The Báb knew that His work on earth was done. He had prepared the people for the coming of the new Messenger of God, and told them to turn to 'Him Whom God Shall Make Manifest'.

What did Bahá'u'lláh do when He had received the Tablet of the Báb from Mullá Husayn? He went about telling people about the Faith of the Báb, just as the Báb had told His followers to do. Who could tell people about the Báb better than Bahá'u'lláh? Everyone in Persia knew that He had not been to school. Nor had He had a famous teacher. Yet He knew more than the divines who had read a great number of books.

Before long many people came to believe in the Báb through Bahá'u'lláh. There were learned men and those who could hardly read or write, rich and poor, farmers and merchants. They became followers of the Báb and they also did what He had told them to do. They went and told other people about His coming. In this way the number of the Báb's followers grew and grew.

But alas, there were also people who did not want to believe in Him and who did not even want to know about Him. And do you know what the strange thing was? These were often the 'ulamá, the learned doctors of religion who used to explain the meaning of the Qur'án to the people: the very ones who should have known better!

The 'ulamá told the authorities bad things about Bahá'u'lláh. They told the Sháh that through Him unrest and rebellion would come to the land. They carried on telling their lies until one day the Sháh said he had decided to have Bahá'u'lláh killed. Muḥammad Sháh told his minister to see that Bahá'u'lláh was taken prisoner, that He should be brought to Ṭihrán.

Bahá'u'lláh was at a seaport when He heard that the Sháh wanted to put Him in prison. In the harbour lay a Russian ship. His friends told Him that He should take the ship and go to Russia so that the Sháh could not harm Him! But Bahá'u'lláh would not flee. He would not hide Himself from those who wished Him harm. He just remained where He was.

15

Next day, Bahá'u'lláh was invited to a party. He went as if nothing was the matter. Suddenly a rider arrived who reported that the Sháh was dead. Now the soldiers could no longer imprison Bahá'u'lláh. Muḥammad Sháh's orders were no longer in force.

Bahá'u'lláh made many journeys through the area where He was born so as to tell as many people as possible about the Báb. Once, on one of these journeys, Bahá'u'lláh saw a young man sitting alone on the side of the road. His hair was untidy. He was dressed as a dervish or beggar.

He had lit a fire beside a stream. Over it he was cooking his dinner. While he was eating Bahá'u'lláh went up to him and asked him in a friendly way: 'Tell me, dervish, what is it you are doing?'

'I am eating God,' he answered bluntly. 'I cook God and burn Him up.'

His simple, easy manners and honest and sincere reply impressed Bahá'u'lláh. He smiled as the dervish gave his strange answer. Bahá'u'lláh liked him and stayed talking to him.

Then something very strange happened. Because Bahá'u'lláh had spoken to him, it did not take long for Mustafá – for this was the name of the dervish – to become quite a different person. He suddenly discovered what the truth was. He saw the light of God, about Whom this kind Stranger had told him. Mustafá liked what Baha'u'lláh told him so much that he immediately arose to follow Bahá'u'lláh. He even forgot to take with him the things in which he cooked his food.

His heart burned with love for Bahá'u'lláh. Singing with joy, he walked behind Bahá'u'lláh as He rode on His horse. 'Thou art the Guiding Star,' was the song he sang; 'Thou art the Light of Truth. Make Thyself known to the people, O Revealer of the Truth.' In this way, Mustafá honoured Bahá'u'lláh because he loved Him so much.

The songs Mustafá sang then became familiar to many. But no one understood exactly what their meaning was. Except for Mustafá, the people did not yet know Who Bahá'u'lláh was. That He was a Messenger of God was still a secret.

7

Bahá'u'lláh in the Síyáh-Chál (I)

Do you know how people in our country are treated when they are in prison? As well as possible, of course. They get enough to eat, they have a bed and their cell is heated if the weather is cold. They are in prison because they deserve to be punished. The judge has decided exactly how much punishment they should have and how long they must stay in prison. Care is taken that they do not get too little punishment and the judge also makes sure that they do not get too much. People in prison in this country are treated justly.

At the time of the Báb and Bahá'u'lláh in Persia things were very different. Prisoners were treated badly, the prisons were cold and dirty, the food was bad and often the prisoners got nothing to eat.

It was even possible to be put in prison without having done anything wrong. This is what happened to many of the Báb's followers. They had not even appeared before a judge who should have decided whether they had broken the Persian laws or not. They were badly treated and many of them were tortured or killed. Why? Because they believed that the Báb was a new Messenger of God.

These persecutions made the life of the Bábís terribly difficult. They became discouraged: their leaders were gone, the Báb had been executed, every day they themselves could be arrested and thrown into prison or

killed. Because of all these troubles some of them really did not know what they were doing any more.

This was the case with a young follower of the Báb who had seen Him being executed in Tabríz. He and a few of his friends wanted to take revenge. They attacked the Sháh and shot at him. Luckily there were no bullets in the gun, but a round of shot which only wounded Náṣiri'd-Dín Sháh slightly.

This attempt upon the life of the Sháh had terrible consequences for the Bábís. Because one of them had done something wrong, all the Bábís had to suffer. Each day more Bábís were sought, each day more were tortured and killed. They had had nothing to do with the attack on the Sháh. You can see how unjust things were at that time in Persia. The Bábís did not even have the chance to prove that they were innocent. The enemies of the Faith did everything they could to take revenge. They also wanted to put Bahá'u'lláh in prison because they thought He was the leader of the Bábís.

When Bahá'u'lláh's friends heard about the attempt on the life of the Sháh, they wanted to help Him to escape. Bahá'u'lláh would not do that. He knew He was safe in God's hands. He did not want to escape from people. He even went willingly to the camp of the Sháh at the time that they were making plans there to take Him prisoner. You can imagine how astonished these people were: the Person they wanted to take prisoner had come to them of His own accord.

From the camp of the Sháh they took Bahá'u'lláh to the Síyáh-Chál in Ṭihrán, the capital of Persia. The Síyáh-Chál was an infamous prison: if you landed in it, things were looking very bad for you. Bahá'u'lláh had to walk in bare feet, bound with chains and bare-headed in the burning sun more than twenty kilometres to the prison. People stood at the side of the road, mocking Him and throwing stones at Him.

The Síyáh-Chál was an underground dungeon which had once been a reservoir for water. You went into it through a dark passageway and then the prisoners had to go down three steep flights of stairs. The dungeon was wrapped in thick darkness and its floor was covered in filth. It had a foul smell. Rats and mice infested the place. There were about one hundred and fifty other prisoners, some of whom were Bábís.

Bahá'u'lláh's feet and those of His companions were placed in stocks. Around Bahá'u'lláh's neck was placed a heavy chain which weighed fifty kilos. Day and night this hung on His neck and shoulders, cutting into them and leaving scars which remained for the rest of His life. For the first three days and nights Bahá'u'lláh was given nothing to eat or drink.

There were many other Bábís with Bahá'u'lláh in that Black Hole. What did they do in that dungeon? You can hardly imagine it under such circumstances, but they began to sing! They chanted a song which Bahá'u'lláh had taught them: a song in which they glorified God and expressed their trust in Him. Their chanting was so loud that it penetrated the walls of the dungeon. It could even be heard in the palace of the Sháh.

'What is the meaning of that sound?' the Sháh asked his servants.

'It is the Bábís singing in their prison,' he was told.

But the Sháh did nothing to set the innocent prisoners free.

8

Bahá'u'lláh in the Síyáh-Chál (II)

Do you remember what it was like in the Black Hole in which Bahá'u'lláh was a prisoner? It was pitch dark, the feet of the prisoners were in stocks, Bahá'u'lláh had a fifty-kilo chain around His neck and it was cold and dirty down there.

Bahá'u'lláh's family prepared food for Him. They asked the prison guards if they might take it to Him. At first the guards would not hear of it but when the family kept insisting, they allowed it to be taken to Bahá'u'lláh. The family was never sure, however, whether He Himself ate it. What did Bahá'u'lláh do? He, Who was hungry Himself, gave the food to fellow prisoners who were almost dying of hunger.

One night in that prison, Bahá'u'lláh was awakened by Mírzá 'Abdu'l-Vahháb from Shíráz. This man was bound to Him by heavy chains. He had had a dream and he wanted to tell it to Bahá'u'lláh. He said that in his dream he had been floating in a space which was infinitely big and beautiful. It was as if he had been carried on wings and could go wherever he pleased. A feeling of passionate delight filled his being. He had glided through this immeasurable space with such speed and ease as he could not describe.

Bahá'u'lláh told 'Abdu'l-Vahháb that it would be his turn that very day to offer his life for his Faith.

Bahá'u'lláh promised him that if he remained steadfast to the end, he would find himself in that unending space of which he had dreamed; with the same speed and ease he would reach the kingdom of immortal sovereignty.

As happened every day, one of the prison guards came that day too to fetch one of the Bábís to put him to death. What do you think? Whose name was called? The name of 'Abdu'l-Vahháb!

At the time that Bahá'u'lláh was in that horrid, dark prison, something very special happened to Him. One night, in a dream, Bahá'u'lláh heard wonderful words coming from every side. They told Him that He would triumph, that He need not be afraid because of what had happened and that He was in safety. In this dark dungeon, the Síyáh-<u>Ch</u>ál, God announced to Bahá'u'lláh that He was the new divine Messenger that the Báb had so often said would come soon. In a Tablet which He later revealed, Bahá'u'lláh has described this tremendous event for us:

'While engulfed in tribulations I heard a most wondrous, a most sweet voice, calling above My head. Turning My face, I beheld a Maiden – the embodiment of the remembrance of the name of My Lord – suspended in the air before Me. So rejoiced was she in her very soul that her countenance shone with the ornament of the good-pleasure of God, and her cheeks glowed with the brightness of the All-Merciful. Betwixt earth and heaven she was raising a call which captivated the hearts and minds of men. She was imparting to both My inward and outer being tidings which rejoiced My soul, and the souls of God's honoured servants. Pointing with her finger unto My head, she addressed all who are in heaven and all who are on earth, saying:

"By God! This is the Best-Beloved of the worlds, and yet ye comprehend not. This is the Beauty of God amongst you, and the power of His sovereignty within you, could ye but understand. This is the Mystery of God and His Treasure, the Cause of God and His glory unto all who are in the kingdoms of Revelation and of creation, if ye be of them that perceive." '

In this vision, God had announced to Bahá'u'lláh that He was secure. But to the outer eye there was not much sign of this. The Sháh's mother wanted revenge for the attack upon her son. She was not satisfied with the death of all the Bábís who had already been killed. She thought that Bahá'u'lláh had plotted the attack and she kept urging the authorities to put Him to death. The enemies of the Faith did their best to help her in this. They wanted to get into her good books. And so what did they do? One day when the food the family had prepared for Bahá'u'lláh was brought to the prison, the enemies secretly mixed some poison with it. Bahá'u'lláh ate the poisoned food and became very ill, but He did not die. His good health was impaired for years because of it.

The enemies also asked a young Bábí named 'Azím whether Bahá'u'lláh had been the leader of the group who had made the attempt on the Sháh. But 'Azím replied that it was he who had urged another youth to assassinate the Sháh. He said he had ardently longed for it as revenge for the death of the Báb. You can guess what happened to 'Azím then: he, too, was killed.

After 'Azím's death, those who wanted revenge for the attack on the Sháh were satisfied to some extent; the cries for vengeance died down. It was also becoming obvious that Bahá'u'lláh had had nothing to do with it. The Prime Minister then sent for Baha'u'lláh, who was still a prisoner in the Black Hole. Someone first offered Bahá'u'lláh fresh clothes, but He would not accept them. Bahá'u'lláh went straight to the Government Building in the clothes which were filthy from the conditions in the prison.

Do you know the first thing the Prime Minister dared to say to Bahá'u'lláh? If Bahá'u'lláh had followed his advice earlier and not got involved with the Faith of the Báb, He would not have been treated so unworthily. Bahá'u'lláh immediately replied that if the Minister had listened to Him, the Government's affairs would not be in such a state as they were.

Then the Minister asked what he should do. Bahá'u'lláh told him that he should order the governors of the land not to persecute the innocent Bábís any longer, nor plunder their houses nor harm their children any more.

That very day orders were given that these cruel, shameful deeds must stop. The Minister wrote that it was now enough. People must stop persecuting and imprisoning the Bábís. And so the dreadful persecutions stopped at last. Bahá'u'lláh had brought this about immediately He was released from the Síyáh-Chál.

9

To Baghdád

How happy His family was when Bahá'u'lláh was released. Now at least He was back home with them again.

For Navváb, the wife of Bahá'u'lláh, and the children, it had been a terrible time. Every day a Bábí had been taken out of the prison and put to death. Navváb knew only too well that every day it could be her Husband.

The enemies of the Faith had made life very difficult for her after they had thrown Bahá'u'lláh into prison. She and the children had been put out of the large and beautiful house in which they lived. The family's possessions had been stolen or destroyed. Their friends and servants were afraid and had nearly all left them. Navváb had only been able to take very little with her and she had had to sell that. With the money she had received she had paid the prison guards to take food to Bahá'u'lláh. They would not have done so unless they had been given payment.

On His release, Bahá'u'lláh went to stay at the house of a cousin, Maryam. He was very ill. As we know, they had tried to poison Him in prison and the heavy chain around His neck had left deep and painful wounds. Maryam and Navváb looked after Him as best they could. But Bahá'u'lláh was hardly out of prison when a new calamity descended on Him and His family. The

Sháh ordered them to leave Persia; within a month they must be out of Ṭihrán. However, Bahá'u'lláh Himself was left to decide to which country they would go.

When the Russian Consul heard that Bahá'u'lláh must leave the country he suggested that He should come to Russia. There, He could live freely and unmolested. The same consul had also done his very best, while Bahá'u'lláh was still in the Síyáh-Chál, to get Him released. Now this person wanted to help Him again. He offered Bahá'u'lláh the protection of the Russian Government and placed at His disposal whatever He might need for the journey to Russia.

Would Bahá'u'lláh accept this offer? If He said 'yes', His life would become much easier. But when Bahá'u'lláh was shut up in the Black Hole He had often thought about the deeds of the Bábís and their situation. He wondered how such noble and intelligent people could ever have brought themselves to attack the Sháh. In the prison Bahá'u'lláh had decided to devote Himself whole-heartedly to the task of re-educating the Bábís. In His unfathomable wisdom, Bahá'u'lláh then chose to go to Baghdád and not to Russia.

In summer Persia is a hot country. But not in the winter. Then it can be dreadfully cold, especially in the mountains. And it was right in the midst of a hard winter that Bahá'u'lláh and His family had to make their journey to Baghdád. They could not even buy enough clothing to protect themselves properly against the cold.

So they set out in the middle of winter, in January, across the snow-covered mountains on their way to Baghdád. Bahá'u'lláh was still sick. The time had been too short for Him to recover from the suffering in that terrible prison. Later, when He was almost at the end of

His earthly life, Bahá'u'lláh wrote about this journey. It was made, He wrote, 'at a time when the cold is so intense that one cannot even speak, and ice and snow so abundant that it is impossible to move.'

Bahá'u'lláh told no one about the vision in the Síyáh-Chál in which the Maiden had appeared to Him. Yet people said that He had changed greatly. A power radiated from Him which had never been seen before. People saw this without being able to understand it.

Some very loyal and devoted followers had become vaguely aware of the transformation in Bahá'u'lláh and the great secret within Him. They wanted to tell everyone. But Bahá'u'lláh would not let them. He ordered them not to speak of it yet. The time had not yet come to do this. It was ten long years before it could be told to the people. You know, I'm sure, the name of the Garden in which Bahá'u'lláh announced that He was God's Messenger for this age. It was the Garden of Riḍván!

Bahá'u'lláh had now left Persia, the country of His birth, forever. He would not return. The enemies of the Faith thought that things would now be calm in Persia and that the Faith of the Báb had come to an end. But they were mistaken. Just by banishing Bahá'u'lláh, Náṣiri'd-Dín Sháh had helped to carry out God's Plan. After all, no one can hold that back. The banishment of Bahá'u'lláh caused the Faith to spread throughout the world with greater power than ever.

10

Bahá'u'lláh's Sorrow

Do you remember what Bahá'u'lláh had resolved to do once He left the prison? – to re-educate the Bábís. He set about doing this in Baghdád.

The Bábís were having a very hard time. The Báb had been executed in Tabríz. Mullá Ḥusayn, Quddús, Ṭáhirih and many other leaders had been killed. There was really no one to whom they could turn for advice. In a short time they had changed a great deal. In the beginning, after the Báb's Declaration, they were noble, honest people who would give anything for their Faith, even their lives. Many Bábís had died as martyrs. But now they were afraid; they met only very secretly.

They were also divided. The unity which they should have had was almost gone. The Báb had prophesied that 'He Whom God shall make manifest' would soon come. This was Bahá'u'lláh but this could not yet be made known. During this time various people came forward and said that they were the One promised by the Báb. The unfortunate Bábís were even more confused by this.

When Bahá'u'lláh arrived in Baghdád from Ṭihrán He was seriously ill; so ill, in fact, that some thought He might die. Fortunately, He got better. As soon as He could, Bahá'u'lláh began to teach and to encourage the believers and advise them. Very soon, Bahá'u'lláh was enjoying a high respect which became greater day by day. He grew to have more and more friends and admirers, one of whom was the governor of Baghdád himself.

It made those who loved Bahá'u'lláh very happy that He was so much honoured. But there were those, too, who did not like it. They were jealous! One of these was Mírzá Yahyá.

Mírzá Yahyá was Bahá'u'lláh's younger half-brother. When their father had died, Mírzá Yahyá was about nine. Bahá'u'lláh had then looked after him like a father.

When the Báb was alive He had appointed Mírzá Yahyá to lead the Bábí community. The Báb did not do this because Yahyá was a suitable person to lead the Faith. He did it to distract the attention of the enemies of the Faith away from Bahá'u'lláh. The Báb knew Who Bahá'u'lláh was and He wanted His life to be saved. After all, it was a time when thousands of Bábís were being killed for their faith.

The Báb Himself knew that Mírzá Yahyá was not a suitable person to lead the Bábís. This was soon obvious, because when Mírzá Yahyá heard of the martyrdom of the Báb, he fled into the mountains. When he went out among the people, he disguised himself so that no one would know who he was. If people came to him with questions, he could not answer them properly. Deeply disappointed, they would then go home again.

Yet Mírzá Yahyá persisted in wanting to be the leader of the Bábís. He tried to persuade them to recognise him as their leader. But the followers of the Báb knew better. They paid hardly any attention to Mírzá Yahyá. He gave himself notions. But they had known for quite some time that he could never be their leader. This made Mírzá

Yaḥyá all the more envious. He tried to sow dissension among the Bábís. He also told them bad things about Bahá'u'lláh which were not true at all.

Bahá'u'lláh suffered a great deal from enemies outside of the Faith. There was hardly anything they did not do to persecute the followers and destroy the Faith! But Bahá'u'lláh suffered far, far more from those who said they were believers but who worked as much as they could against Him. They did this because they were ambitious or jealous. They wanted an honour which did not belong to them or they wanted to be the leader, even though they were not capable of leading anyone. No one will ever understand how much sorrow Bahá'u'lláh had because of this. Bahá'u'lláh Himself once wrote that His sorrow over what Mírzá Yaḥyá had done was greater than the sorrow of a mother whose child has died.

Bahá'u'lláh sensed that much worse things might happen. Therefore He decided to leave Baghdád. And one morning when His family awoke they found that He had disappeared. No one knew where He had gone.

11

Alone in the Wilderness

Far away, high in the mountains, there lived a man alone, a dervish. Where He had come from no one knew. He called himself Darvísh Muḥammad. They did know that He was very kind to everyone. If He saw that someone was sad, He would at once go to help him.

Once He saw a boy sitting at the side of the road, weeping. He wanted to comfort him and asked him why he was crying.

'Oh Sir!' replied the boy. 'The master punished me because my writing is so bad. I can't write and now I've no copy either. I don't dare go back to school . . .'

'Don't cry any more,' said the dervish. 'I will write a piece for you and show you how to copy it. Then you can show it to your master.'

When the boy's teacher saw how beautifully the copy was written he was absolutely amazed. He had never seen such beautiful handwriting.

'Who gave you this?' the master asked the boy.

'The dervish on the mountain wrote it for me.'

'Whoever wrote that is not a dervish but a king,' said the master.

You have already guessed, of course, that we are talking about Bahá'u'lláh. When He left His house in Baghdád, in the middle of the night, without anyone seeing Him, one of His servants went with Him. But the

33

servant was killed by robbers soon afterwards and Bahá'u'lláh was left alone. He went a long way into the desert until He found an area where hardly anyone lived. A few peasants came there twice a year: in spring, to sow, and at the end of the summer to harvest.

Bahá'u'lláh spent most of His time on the top of a mountain. There He lived in a stone hut which the peasants used to shelter in when the weather was very bad.

It was a difficult time for Bahá'u'lláh. It happened more than once that He had nothing to eat. He was also very sorrowful, especially because of what Mírzá Yaḥyá had done. Years later, Bahá'u'lláh wrote about this time in the

Book of Certitude: 'From Our eyes there rained tears of anguish, and in Our bleeding heart there surged an ocean of agonising pain. Many a night We had no food . . . and many a day Our body found no rest.'

And yet . . . in spite of all the tribulations and difficulties, Bahá'u'lláh felt very happy. He has written that His soul was filled with an unspeakable joy. For in His loneliness, His enemies could not embitter His life. He was very close to God and this often made Him so happy that He forgot the world around Him.

Do you think that it was possible for Bahá'u'lláh to remain unnoticed in that lonely spot where very few people lived? Would no one discover sooner or later that the lonely Darvísh Muhammad was a very special Person?

Just imagine a room which is pitch dark, so dark that you cannot see your hand before your face. Then someone lights a lamp in that room. All at once everything is different. Then you can see where the tables and chairs are, you see the pictures on the wall and many other things. Lighting the lamp has changed the whole room. And what can you see best of all? – the lamp itself!

This is what it was like when Bahá'u'lláh lived in that lonesome wilderness. His divine light could not remain hidden. Someone who lived in a house nearby discovered Him after dreaming about the Prophet Muhammad. He told some of the leaders in the town of Sulaymáníyyih about it. One of them went to see Bahá'u'lláh and, after long persuasion, succeeded in getting Him to come and live in the town.

In the beginning no one thought that Darvísh Muhammad had any special wisdom or knowledge. He spoke little and kept to Himself. But this soon changed.

Students and scholars then began to come to Him to ask Him questions. He could answer even the most difficult questions about which they had meditated for years. They sat in silent admiration. And when He had written a poem which was even finer and better than the poems of the famous Ibnu'l-Fárid, they were completely convinced of His greatness.

Now all kinds of people came to visit Him: Kurds, Persians, Arabs, scholars and those who could scarcely read or write, rich and poor. They loved to be in His presence and to hear Him speak. And if they had any problems they would tell Him, and Darvísh Muḥammad would show them the way to solve them. The people wanted Him to stay in Sulaymáníyyih forever. But would this be possible?

12

Home Again at Last

It was now quite a long time since Bahá'u'lláh had left His home without telling anyone. His family still did not know where He was. Navváb, Bahá'u'lláh's wife, and their children Bahá'íyyih <u>Kh</u>ánum and 'Abdu'l-Bahá, were very sad.

But there was someone who was not sad because Bahá'u'lláh had left. That was Mírzá Yaḥyá. After all, he wanted the Bábís to see him as their leader and not Bahá'u'lláh. And now Bahá'u'lláh was away, he had the chance.

Bahá'u'lláh knew well that Mírzá Yaḥyá would be pleased. Much later, He explained why He had gone away. His departure was a test. If Mírzá Yaḥyá were the real leader then that would become clear and he would then be able to lead the Bábís. They would then take their troubles to Mírzá Yaḥyá and he would help them to solve their problems. But could Mírzá Yaḥyá really be the leader of the Bábís?

Mírzá Yaḥyá lived in the house of Bahá'u'lláh's family. They did everything they could to please him because this is what Bahá'u'lláh had asked them to do. But he was an ungrateful man. He always made remarks about the food. And he never gave a helping hand in the home; not even with the heavy work, like getting water from the well. He left that to Navváb and young Bahá'íyyih even though they hardly had the strength to pull up the heavy bucket of water.

Mírzá Yaḥyá was frightened. He was afraid that he would be taken and thrown into prison. He only thought of his own safety. Bahá'íyyih was never allowed out to play with the children in the neighbourhood. Her little brother, who had been born a few months after they arrived in Baghdád, became very ill. But Mírzá Yaḥyá would not allow anyone to come to see him, not even the doctor. And when the little boy died, they were not allowed to arrange the funeral. They had to give his body to a man and they never knew where the child was buried.

When they moved to another house, Mírzá Yaḥyá did not dare to go with them. He was much too afraid that he would be seen and he went to live in a tiny house on his own. They were rather glad to be rid of him.

It was very soon obvious that Mírzá Yaḥyá was not a good leader. Instead of leading people to God he taught them evil deeds. He even had Mírzá 'Alí-Akbar, a cousin of the Báb, murdered. He told the Bábís that at night they should steal the belongings of the Muslim pilgrims who arrived in the area.

The Bábís were no longer in agreement with each other. They were divided. In a short time they had such a bad reputation that they were openly abused. They were a disgrace. They hardly dared to go out any more. So it was clear that Mírzá Yaḥyá would never manage to inspire new life into the Faith or give the Bábís new hope. No, in fact the exact opposite happened!

The family and faithful friends of Bahá'u'lláh longed more and more for His return. Where could He possibly be? Wherever they could, they tried to find out something

about Him. But they always failed. 'Abdu'l-Bahá in particular missed his Father. He was terribly sad because of His disappearance. Once he prayed the same prayer all night long for his Father's return to them.

The next day, 'Abdu'l-Bahá and his uncle Mírzá Músá met two people who told them about a wondrous Person who lived as a dervish in the desert mountains of Sulaymáníyyih. They called Him the 'Nameless One'. Because of His love, everyone in that area had come to love Him. When they heard this, 'Abdu'l-Bahá and Mírzá Músá knew at once that the dervish must be Bahá'u'lláh!

Two faithful friends went on the journey to seek Bahá'u'lláh. When they arrived in Sulaymáníyyih they noticed how the people there respected Him. Even the cleverest people came to Him to listen to His wise lessons and to ask Him for advice. These people became very upset when they heard that Darvísh Muḥammad would be leaving them.

'Oh Master,' they said. 'Shall we never see You again?'

Bahá'u'lláh reassured them and told them that they could come to visit Him in Baghdád.

In great excitement, the family waited in Baghdád after they heard that their Father would soon be home again. Navváb made a splendid coat for Him of costly red Persian material. It was one of the few things she still had left from her trousseau.

At last, at long last, He came. They heard footsteps and a moment later a dervish walked in. Through the disguise they could see that it was their Father.

How happy they were that He was back! 'Abdu'l-Bahá was perhaps the happiest of them all. He all but hid himself in his Father's clothing, so closely did he cling to Him. He caught His hand and held it tight. It was as if he would never let Him go.

13

The Great Change

It could have been a splendid garden. The best gardener in the world worked in it. The most beautiful flowers could have bloomed in it. But alas, there was someone who was jealous, who thought that *he* was the best gardener. At night he went to destroy the work of the real gardener; he trampled on the flowers, pulled up the seedlings and scattered weeds everywhere. This made

the real gardener very sad. He could not work like that. He thought: 'If the other one thinks he can do better than I can, let him try it.' So he went away.

The bad gardener was now left to his own devices. But do you think he could do the job? Of course not; he could not manage it at all. In a very short time the garden was in a dreadful mess. No one came to look at it. It had turned into a wilderness.

Then the people wished that the real gardener would come back. After searching for a long time they found him and asked if he would look after the garden once again.

The real gardener got a shock when he saw the wilderness which he had wanted to make into a splendid garden. He went to work at once. It was not long before the garden began to change. The first lovely, fragrant flowers came into bloom. Soon the garden was much tidier. The weeds disappeared and more and more beautiful flowers and shrubs grew in it. And the people came again to admire it. More and more of them came. After a few years the garden had become so beautiful and famous that people came from great distances to enjoy it. It had become a place of delight.

This is what happened to the Bábís. When Bahá'u'lláh returned from the mountains of Sulaymáníyyih to Baghdád He saw that the Bábís had lost their faith. This made Him very sad. But He began at once to teach them again and show them the way to God once more. He taught them to be honest, reliable people again.

Less than a year after Bahá'u'lláh's return to Baghdád, the Bábís were once again the ardent believers which they had been in the time of the Báb. Now the people respected them again instead of calling insults after them on the street. They were happy again too, now that they had their Leader back among them.

When the Bábís in Persia heard that Bahá'u'lláh was back in Baghdád, they came to visit Him. Actually this was very strange. Bahá'u'lláh had not yet told anyone that He was the Promised One Whom the Báb had constantly said would soon appear. Yet the Bábís made the dangerous journey to Baghdád to be with Bahá'u'lláh, such was His attraction for them. They felt that He was much more than just an ordinary person.

There were others who also visited Him. These were the scholars from Sulaymáníyyih. They had come to know Bahá'u'lláh when He lived in their city as a dervish. They had often listened to Him and brought their problems to Him. They had been very sorry when Bahá'u'lláh had left them. But fortunately He had invited them to come to visit Him in Baghdád at the house of Mírzá Músá the Bábí. And He had only just got back to Baghdád when they began to arrive.

All these visitors made the inhabitants of Baghdád very curious. They wondered who it was that the visitors were coming to see. They went to have a look and it was not long before many people from Baghdád were being drawn to Bahá'u'lláh as by a magnet. Even the learned of Baghdád came to visit Him and ask Him questions. The answers given by Bahá'u'lláh were so brilliant that they became His admirers. Even princes came to visit Him. And the British Consul who represented his country in Baghdád wrote letters to Bahá'u'lláh and offered Him his protection. He was prepared to pass on any message which Bahá'u'lláh might want to address to Queen Victoria.

Bahá'u'lláh had a tremendous influence on people. In

His presence they felt unimaginably happy. He brought out the best in everyone and through Him they developed their good qualities such as kindness, honesty, piety, humility, self-sacrifice. Bahá'u'lláh taught them to submit themselves to the will of God.

The believers, despite their modest earnings, held joyous feasts in honour of Bahá'u'lláh. These were such that even the kings of the earth had never dreamed of anything like them. Believers who had come into close contact with Bahá'u'lláh were so deeply affected and so happy that everything else in the world became unimportant to them.

One of them wrote later about this joyous time:

'Many a night no less than ten persons subsisted on no more than a pennyworth of dates. No one knew to whom actually belonged the shoes, the cloaks, or the robes that were to be found in their houses. Whoever went to the bazaar could claim that the shoes upon his feet were his own, and each one who entered the presence of Bahá'u'lláh could affirm that the cloak and robe he then wore belonged to him. Their own names they had forgotten, their hearts were emptied of aught else except adoration for their Beloved . . . O, for the joy of those days, and the gladness and wonder of those hours!'

How much had changed since Bahá'u'lláh had returned. There was now no trace of the disorder which had been created in the time that Mírzá Yaḥyá was supposed to lead the Faith. It was quite obvious to the Bábís Who their true leader was. There could no longer be any possible doubt!

14

The Book of Certitude (I)

Ḥájí Mírzá Siyyid Muḥammad just could not believe it. Of course he could see that his Nephew was a very special Person. But to believe that his sister's Son was the Qá'im, the Promised One the followers of Muḥammad had been awaiting for such a long time, for Whose coming they prayed every day – that was too much for him.

It was a different matter for his brother Ḥájí Mírzá Siyyid 'Alí. As soon as he knew that the Báb had declared Himself to be a Messenger of God, he had become one of His followers. He had lovingly devoted the rest of his life to the new Faith. A few months before the Báb was executed in Tabríz, this uncle of the Báb had sacrificed his own life for the Cause.

Naturally Ḥájí Mírzá Siyyid Muḥammad was very sad about what had happened to the members of his family. His brother and his Nephew had both been killed. His sister, the Báb's mother, had gone to live in far-off Iraq because she could no longer stand living in Shíráz where she had lived with her Son.

He often talked about the claim of the Báb to other people, including the Bábís, who then tried to remove his doubts. People kept trying to convince him that his Nephew was the promised Qá'im. Until one of the Báb's followers said that the same thing had happened in the

45

time of Muḥammad: one of Muḥammad's uncles also could not believe that his Nephew was a Messenger of God; yet it was true. The follower of the Báb then said to Ḥájí Mírzá Siyyid Muḥammad that he should investigate for himself whether or not the Báb was a Messenger of God. After all, God was able to make his Nephew the promised Qá'ím, wasn't He?

Ḥájí Mírzá Siyyid Muḥammad was very moved by these words. 'What shall I do now?' he asked.

The believer with whom he was conversing suggested that he should go to Baghdád and pay a visit to Bahá'u'lláh. He agreed that this was the best thing to do.

When he went to see Bahá'u'lláh, he was lovingly received. Ḥájí Mírzá Siyyid Muḥammad felt how good it was to be in the presence of Bahá'u'lláh. He wrote to his son that he would like to stay with Him forever. Again and again, the words of Bahá'u'lláh made him very happy. He asked Bahá'u'lláh to explain the truth about the Message of the Báb. Bahá'u'lláh agreed to his request. He asked the Báb's uncle to make a list of all the questions which he would like answered. Ḥájí Mírzá Siyyid Muḥammad started right away and by the next day he had written down all his questions.

Bahá'u'lláh gave detailed answers to the questions. In less than two days and two nights He had revealed a book almost 260 pages long. Bahá'u'lláh later called it the *Kitáb-i-Íqán*. In English we call it the *Book of Certitude*.

In this book, Bahá'u'lláh explains how it comes about that every time a new Messenger from God appears people refuse to accept Him. Moses was rejected by the Egyptians, Jesus by the Jews and it took a long time for the Arabs to believe in Muḥammad. The people say that they are longing for the coming of the new Promised

One. They even pray to God to send Him quickly. But when He comes they do not believe in Him.

When a new Messenger of God appears, things are always different from what is expected. People want Him to say the things they want to hear, and to do things according to their expectations. The Jews wanted Jesus to liberate them from the Romans who had conquered Israel; they really wanted Him to be an earthly king.

A Messenger of God looks like an ordinary person who eats, drinks and sleeps. When they see Him, most people see nothing special about Him. They wonder how such a person could be sent by God. He looks just like themselves, doesn't He? Surely He cannot be sent by God to lead people and bring them back to God. So they turn away from Him because He is not as they themselves had expected. They even go much further: they say He is an unbeliever because He does not keep the laws which have been valid in their country for hundreds of years. Then they persecute Him; sometimes they even put Him to death!

Bahá'u'lláh explains in the *Book of Certitude* that people must become seekers after Truth. They must not follow others blindly, or believe automatically what other people say or let themselves be led in the wrong direction by their criticism. Anyone who seeks the Truth must put his trust in God. Then the difference between truth and lies will be just as clear to him as the difference between light and shadow.

15

The Book of Certitude (II)

Just try to imagine what it would be like if the sun never shone again. What would the earth look like?

It would be dark and cold. Trees, flowers, fruits and animals would no longer be able to grow. They would get no more light or warmth and everything would die. In a short time there would be no living being left. The earth would become a dead planet.

What would it be like for people if God had not sent His Messengers? Then we would not know how to live. Because, just as the visible sun helps the trees and plants on earth to grow, the Messengers of God, with their knowledge and love, also help people to develop. They are the Educators of mankind.

The Messengers are sources of love for mankind. They love us more than anyone else on this earth. Through Them we learn that we must love God. And that we must love each other.

The Messengers of God are also sources of knowledge for mankind. Through Them we learn to know God. For God is so great and so exalted that we ordinary people cannot get to know Him by ourselves. Because God wants us to know Him, He sends His Messengers. These Messengers have divine Knowledge. Even the cleverest people in this world cannot ever hope to equal Them. Nor do the Messengers of God tell mankind all They know by any means. People would not be able to bear it. They tell mankind all that it needs to know for that age and no more.

You could compare the knowledge They possess with a great ocean. This great ocean is the treasure house of the Knowledge of God. From this ocean They take a drop of knowledge and reveal that to mankind. That one drop from the ocean of Knowledge can completely change the lives of the people who listen. People give up their old habits, their fear turns into courage, their unease into tranquillity and their doubts into certainty. All these riches are given to those who believe in the Messenger of God.

Bahá'u'lláh tells the story in the *Book of Certitude* of a poor man who complained about his poverty to Ṣádiq, a leader of the Muslim religion. Ṣádiq then told him that he was very rich.

The poor man was astonished when he heard this and said: 'Where are my riches? I don't even possess a penny.'

'Do you not possess my love?' asked Ṣádiq.

He answered: 'Oh yes, I possess that, O descendant of God's Prophet!'

And Ṣádiq then asked him: 'Would you exchange this love for a thousand dinars?'

He replied: 'No, I would never exchange it even if the whole world and all that is in it were given to me.'

Then Ṣádiq observed: 'How can he who possesses such a treasure be called poor?'

In the *Book of Certitude* we can find an example of how to teach the Faith. Ḥájí Mírzá Siyyid Muḥammad had asked Bahá'u'lláh to explain the truth about the Báb to him. Bahá'u'lláh, in this book which is His reply, does not prove straight away that the Báb is the promised Qá'im. He first speaks of the other Prophets, who have come one after another, of the history of religion and its oneness. He gives the meaning of difficult passages in the Bible and the Qur'án and explains the reason why most of the people have failed to recognise the Messenger of God when He has appeared. Bahá'u'lláh proves the truth and authority of Christ and Muḥammad.

Not until the very end of the book does Bahá'u'lláh write about the Báb. He reminds Ḥájí Mírzá Siyyid Muḥammad how the followers of the Báb were persecuted and gave up their possessions and their lives for the new Faith, just like the followers of Christ and Muḥammad had.

The Báb was a Youth of twenty-five when He founded His Faith. Innumerable people worked against Him and yet they could not hold back the Message taught by this one Youth. Was this not a proof of His divine power? Again and again, Bahá'u'lláh urges Ḥájí Mírzá Siyyid Muḥammad to meditate on this: then he will understand how great the Revelation of the Báb is.

Fortunately, the Báb's uncle gave the words of Bahá'u'-lláh some thought. When he had read the *Book of Certitude* he no longer had any doubts. He now recognised that the Báb was a Messenger of God. He believed with absolute certainty.

16

The Enemies Have Their Way After All

More and more people came to visit Bahá'u'lláh when He lived in Baghdád. They came from all kinds of backgrounds: learned men from Sulaymáníyyih, Bábís from Persia, religious leaders of Baghdád, members of the government and even princes. All of them were attracted to Bahá'u'lláh as if by a magnet and they all wanted to visit His hospitable house. Even the governor of Baghdád came to visit Him in person in order to show his respect.

When He lived in Baghdád, Bahá'u'lláh often left His house. He would go to visit the believers or for a walk along the banks of the River Tigris. The believers were often worried when Bahá'u'lláh walked through the streets of Baghdád. They thought it was really too dangerous for Him. They were afraid that He might be killed.

It was very understandable that they were afraid of this, because there were some people who wanted Bahá'u'lláh to be killed. It was a thorn in their side that everyone paid Him so much attention and respected Him so highly. Bahá'u'lláh knew well what plans some of them had. But no matter how much His followers and loved ones warned Him and begged Him, He still went into the city without anyone accompanying Him for protection. And if He saw the people that He knew wished to harm Him, he would go up to them. This really embarrassed them. They were deeply ashamed and decided not to carry out their plans.

One of those who wanted to try to kill Bahá'u'lláh was Riḍá, a bandit. The Consul-General had hired him for a large sum of money. He was given a horse and two pistols to go in search of Bahá'u'lláh and assassinate Him.

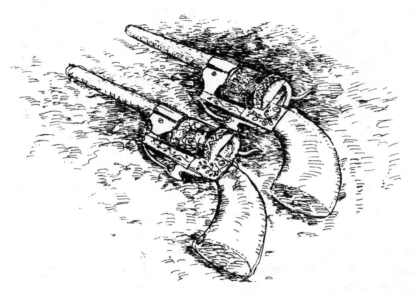

'And', the Consul-General assured the bandit, 'you need not be afraid you will be put in prison. I will make sure that does not happen.'

So the bandit began to look for a suitable opportunity. Where would he carry out his evil plans? One day, he found out that Bahá'u'lláh was using the public baths. Some of the Bábís were keeping watch outside. But the bandit managed to get inside the building when they were not looking. He had a pistol under his coat. In a few moments he stood opposite Bahá'u'lláh. Now he had his chance – the chance he had been waiting for for so long. And what happened? . . . He lost his nerve!

Another time the same bandit hid himself and waited for Bahá'u'lláh to pass along the street where he was posted. Again, he waited his chance, with his pistol at the ready. But when Bahá'u'lláh came close, he became so frightened that he dropped his pistol on the ground. Bahá'u'lláh knew what had happened. He told his brother, Mírzá Músá, to give back the gun to the bandit and show him the way to his house.

It was a happy time for the Bábís in Baghdád. Their meetings would go on into the depths of the night when they would sing the praises of the Báb and Bahá'u'lláh in their prayers and songs. It often happened that they were so absorbed in their prayers that they only noticed that the next day had broken when it had been light for quite some time. The devoted followers of Bahá'u'lláh had only one goal: Bahá'u'lláh. Again and again, they sought opportunities to be in His presence. When they had succeeded and were leaving His presence, the first thought they had was: 'How soon can I get to see Him again?' A prince who came to visit Bahá'u'lláh in His room once said: 'I do not know how to explain it but if all the sorrows of the world were weighing on my heart, I have the feeling they would all disappear as soon as one came into the presence of Bahá'u'lláh. It is as if I had stepped into Paradise itself.'

But the enemies remained active. They tried in all kinds of ways to destroy the Faith. For example, they told lies about Bahá'u'lláh and about the Bábís. They annoyed the Bábís in the hope that one of them would become so angry that he would take revenge. But, thanks to

Bahá'u'lláh's leadership, the Bábís did not allow themselves to be tempted into any deeds of vengeance.

The enemies also began writing letters to the Sháh of Persia. What they said about Bahá'u'lláh in these letters was, of course, not the truth. They said that He was a very dangerous person, that He was a threat to the security of Persia and its government. Therefore, they said, it was necessary for Bahá'u'lláh to leave Baghdád. He should go somewhere else, preferably as far away from Persia as possible.

After much insistence and many more letters, they at last got their way: the authorities gave orders to ask Bahá'u'lláh if He would come to Constantinople, which was the capital.

Bahá'u'lláh's exile in Baghdád lasted for ten years. All those years Bahá'u'lláh knew that He was God's Messenger. After all, God had revealed this to Him in the Síyáh-Chál in Ṭihrán. But Bahá'u'lláh had never told anyone. There were some believers who had discovered for themselves that Bahá'u'lláh was the Promised One the Báb had foretold. But Bahá'u'lláh had told them they were not to speak of it to anyone.

It would not be long now before Bahá'u'lláh Himself would make the great announcement. This would happen before He set out on the journey to Constantinople.

17

In the Garden of Riḍván

The news spread like wildfire through Baghdád. 'Did
you know?' 'Where did you hear it?' the people were
asking each other. The news had come that Bahá'u'lláh
was leaving Baghdád. The authorities had asked Him to
go to Constantinople.

The people of Baghdád were very upset. They had
come to love Him very much during all the years He had
lived among them.

The saddest of all were the Bábís. When they heard the
news none of them could sleep the whole night, their
sorrow was so great. Many wept and wept and could not
stop. Others said they would commit suicide unless they
could go to Constantinople too. And they would have
done it if Bahá'u'lláh had not prevented them. He
comforted the people and calmed them down. His words
helped them to submit themselves to the will of God.

News of the departure spread rapidly through Baghdád
and the neighbouring villages. For years it had been the
custom for many people to visit Bahá'u'lláh every day.
But now that they knew He was to leave for Constantinople, there was a great rush to see Him. Countless
visitors came to Him in order to be in His presence one
more time and to honour Him.

The house in which Bahá'u'lláh lived was much too
small for this. When Najíb Páshá, one of the foremost

citizens of Baghdád, heard this, he offered Bahá'u'lláh the Najíbíyyih Garden in which to receive His guests. This was a beautiful garden near Baghdád, on the opposite bank of the River Tigris. The followers later called it the 'Garden of Riḍván'.

When Bahá'u'lláh left His house a few days later to go to this garden, the whole of Baghdád was on the watch. People stood on the flat roofs of their houses to catch a glimpse of Him. Many threw themselves at His feet on the street. They jostled each other just to touch Him for a moment, to hear a few words spoken by Him or just to see His face once more.

One little boy only a few years old ran to Him and clung to His garments. Weeping, he begged Bahá'u'lláh not to leave them. When all the people saw this, their sorrow was increased. Bahá'u'lláh understood perfectly, of course, that His going away was very hard for the people to bear. He comforted them and promised that they should visit Him in the Garden of Riḍván.

During the time that Bahá'u'lláh spent in the Garden of Riḍván something very unusual happened. A secret that had been hidden for ten years was revealed. Bahá'u'lláh told the followers who were with Him that He was the Messenger of God promised by the Báb and by all the Holy Scriptures of the past.

Bahá'u'lláh had known for ten years that He was the Promised One. God had revealed it to Him when He was a prisoner in the Síyáh-Chál, the dark and dirty dungeon in Ṭihrán. In a vision Bahá'u'lláh had seen a Maiden who had told Him that He was secure and that He would triumph. During all those years Bahá'u'lláh had told no one about it. But now that He was leaving Baghdád, the time had come for His station to be revealed.

What joyous news it was for the followers who heard Bahá'u'lláh's announcement that afternoon in the Garden of Riḍván! Bahá'u'lláh Himself also radiated the greatest joy. He knew he was being banished to a strange, faraway country. He knew that His life there would be terribly hard and that He would suffer greatly. And yet, because of this announcement that He was the Messenger of God, these days in the Garden of Riḍván were very happy and were named by Him the 'Most Great Festival'.

We do not actually know how Bahá'u'lláh announced that He was the Promised One the Báb had so often said God would reveal. It was such a mighty event and so thrilling that it must have been indescribable. None of His followers later gave a description of exactly what it was like. Can you imagine such a thing? That anyone can be so happy about something that he can't tell you about it afterwards?

The Garden of Riḍván was very beautiful with its splendid pathways lined with colourful roses in bloom. Very early in the mornings, when it was just getting light, the gardeners used to pick the roses and lay them on the ground in Bahá'u'lláh's tent. Sometimes the pile was so high that the visitors who came to see Bahá'u'lláh could not even see over it. Then Bahá'u'lláh would give the roses to His followers and ask them to take them to Persian or Arab friends in Baghdad.

And the opponents of the Faith? At first they were glad. At long last they had succeeded: Bahá'u'lláh was leaving Baghdád. But this soon changed. They began to regret it bitterly. Everything had turned out so differently from what they had hoped!

The opponents of the Faith had wanted to see Bahá'u'lláh humiliated. But what happened? When He passed through the streets of Baghdád on His way to the Garden of Riḍván He had been cheered by the population as no king had ever been cheered.

The opponents had wanted to destroy the new Faith. But once more, exactly the opposite happened. At that very moment Bahá'u'lláh announced that He was the Messenger of God. At that very moment the greatest feast began, which the Bahá'ís now celebrate every year: the Feast of Riḍván.

This Feast lasts for twelve days: April 21 is the first day and May 2 is the last. Twelve days – the same number of days that Bahá'u'lláh spent in the Garden of Riḍván.

18

Constantinople

How busy it was in Baghdád! The streets were crowded.

This happened every time Bahá'u'lláh went along the street. As soon as people heard that Bahá'u'lláh had gone to town, they hurried out of their houses to catch a glimpse of Him or hear a few of His words of wisdom.

But now . . . now it was busier than ever. The people of Baghdád knew that Bahá'u'lláh was departing for Constantinople. Perhaps they would never see Him again. This was their last chance.

Bahá'u'lláh saddled a horse which His followers had bought for Him. It was a splendid animal, the finest and the best they could buy. The people crowded around Bahá'u'lláh so that the horse could hardly move forward. Many bowed their heads in the dust before its feet and kissed its hooves. Others embraced the stirrups. Sometimes it looked as if the horse would trample on the people kneeling on the road. There were others, too, who tried to walk with it, to pay this last respect to Bahá'u'lláh. And this made it even harder to get through.

The whole of Baghdád was sad. Not only the followers and friends of Bahá'u'lláh, but also His enemies. At first they had done their very best to get rid of Bahá'u'lláh from Baghdád. They were glad they had at last succeeded. But now that they saw how sorrowful the people were that He was going, they would have much preferred Him to stay.

Bahá'u'lláh was a prisoner of the State. But it certainly did not look as if a prisoner were leaving Baghdád. Prisoners are not cheered. People are usually glad when they go. 'At least we're rid of them,' they say. Bahá'u'lláh left Baghdád as a king whose subjects love him very much. And is He not the King of Kings?

So began the journey to Constantinople, a long journey to a far-off city in an unknown land.

Travelling was not easy in those days and certainly not in the area through which Bahá'u'lláh had to go. The roads were rough and full of potholes. Sometimes they were very narrow too, especially in the mountains. Many made the journey on foot. Sometimes they had a kind of chair which was placed on the back of a mule or a horse: howdahs, they are called. Two people could sit in one. They could shade themselves from the burning sun with parasols. But there were also people who walked beside the animals to keep them on the road. No wonder such journeys took a long time.

During Bahá'u'lláh's journey with His companions to Constantinople it was not very different. It took them over a hundred days. Over the mountains and through the valleys of Iraq and Turkey they went, through lonely places where few people lived. Sometimes they travelled for hours without meeting anyone.

'Abdu'l-Bahá and the believers who went with Him to Constantinople surrounded Bahá'u'lláh and His family with great devotion. No trouble was too much for them to undertake in order to make the journey as comfortable as possible. They were so happy that they had not had to stay behind in Baghdád. Now they were with their Beloved every day. For this they were quite willing to make a long and tiring journey.

They were a happy band of travellers. They had a lot of fun during their long journeys. One of the believers, called Jináb-i-Muníb, had a splendid voice. With his songs and prayers, in which he glorified Bahá'u'lláh, he made the company feel even happier and more joyful.

In every town and village Bahá'u'lláh was received like royalty. Feasts were prepared and the most delicious dishes were cooked. Other people had journeyed through these parts but the population had never welcomed anyone who was as kind to them as Bahá'u'lláh. All were attracted to Him.

At last, after more than a hundred days, the exiles arrived at the port of Sámsún. There they boarded a steamer which brought them across the Black Sea to Constantinople in three days. This was much faster than the journey over land.

When Bahá'u'lláh arrived in Constantinople the most difficult period of His earthly life began. He Himself knew quite well what sufferings were in store for Him! He had said so more than once in the Tablets which He had revealed. It would, however, also be the time of the greatest triumphs. The kings and rulers of the world were to hear that God had sent a new Messenger.

19

The Bábís become Bahá'ís

A great many people turned out to say goodbye when Bahá'u'lláh was leaving Baghdád. They were sorrowful because He was leaving. It had been so wonderful listening to Him and it had made people so happy to be near Him.

But hardly anyone yet knew what had happened in the Garden of Riḍván. Not many people knew what Bahá'u'lláh had announced there: that He was God's Messenger for this Age.

Bahá'u'lláh Himself had known this for ten years. During all those years He had told no one. Some people had discovered it for themselves. To these Bahá'u'lláh had said that they must not tell anyone.

When Bahá'u'lláh, His family and some faithful followers arrived in Constantinople, the time had come for the Bábís to be told that Bahá'u'lláh was Him Whom the Báb had promised God would make manifest. Now it need no longer be kept secret.

Bahá'u'lláh knew that it must be done very carefully. The Bábís in Persia were still being persecuted. The enemies were always lying in wait. If a Bábí left his home, he was never sure that he would return. If there was someone who wanted to know more about the Faith, he would go secretly in the middle of the night, so as not to be seen, to visit one of the Bábís.

Once, in the dead of night, two men knocked at the door of Ḥaydar-'Alí, one of Bahá'u'lláh's most loyal followers. The men wanted Ḥaydar-'Alí to tell them about the Faith. When he had spoken with them for several hours, one of the men decided to accept the Faith. The other was not yet sure. He would have to think about it. So Ḥaydar-'Alí gave him the *Book of Certitude* to take with him.

This man used to read in the evenings. But after a while he got frightened; just imagine if anyone should suddenly walk in and find him reading one of the Bábís' books. He might well lose all his possessions as a result; they might even kill him! He stood up, locked the door and tried to go on reading. Then he thought: it is still early in the evening; if anyone came along and discovered that I had locked the door, he would think I was reading one of the Bábís' books. So he decided to go to bed and to sleep. But, he thought then, just imagine if anyone should find out I had gone to bed so early. He would think I was going to get up in the middle of the night to read one of the Bábís' books. Finally, he hid the book in the stable.

The believers in Persia always had to be very careful. Therefore Bahá'u'lláh sent wise and sensible people to Persia to tell the Bábís what had happened in the Garden of Riḍván. One of these was Jináb-i-Muníb who had sung such beautiful songs on the journey from Baghdád to Constantinople.

So he set out once more back to Persia. First he went to Ṭihrán. Cautiously, he told some of the Bábís what had happened in the Garden of Riḍván. Soon afterwards he received a Tablet which Bahá'u'lláh had revealed for him. In this Muníb was ordered to arise and to awaken the Bábís. He then travelled throughout Persia telling the Bábís the news of Bahá'u'lláh's Announcement.

Each time a new Messenger of God appears it is difficult for the followers of the previous Messenger to believe in Him. Was this true of the Bábís? Again and again, the Báb had told them that 'He Whom God shall make manifest' would soon come. The Báb had done everything to prepare people for the coming of Bahá'u'lláh. They knew of Bahá'u'lláh. He was the Leader of the Bábís to Whom they could go with their problems and difficulties. But would they also believe that Bahá'u'lláh was the One the Báb had promised?

Many believed it immediately. But there were some Bábís who could not accept it at once. There were even some who became angry when they heard it, so great wisdom and much patience was needed to explain it to them.

Aḥmad was one of the followers sent by Bahá'u'lláh to Persia to inform the Bábís about 'Him Whom God shall make manifest'. He arrived in a place called Furúgh where Mullá Mírzá Muḥammad and his brothers lived. When Aḥmad told them about Bahá'u'lláh they attacked him and started to fight with him. They gave him such a hard time that one of his teeth was broken.

What did Aḥmad do then? Did he go off in a huff? No! When they stopped fighting and calmed down he went on explaining to them. They began to read some of the Báb's writings together. After a while the brothers saw that Aḥmad was right. They accepted Bahá'u'lláh and became Bahá'ís.

Thanks to the faithful, courageous followers, the good news was made known to all the Bábís in Persia. Some found it hard to believe at first. But after a while nearly all the Bábís accepted Bahá'u'lláh.

The Bábís became Bahá'ís, followers of Bahá'u'lláh. This is what the Báb had wanted!

20

From Constantinople to Adrianople

This was no way to treat people!

It was no way to treat Bahá'u'lláh, His family and a little group of His followers: to banish them in the middle of winter. They had to leave Constantinople as quickly as possible. They were not even given time to buy warm clothing.

What had happened?

When Bahá'u'lláh had arrived in Constantinople after the long journey from Baghdád, He was received like a king. Many people came to visit Him and do Him honour, even government ministers! They thought that Bahá'u'lláh needed them and that He would ask them to help Him, or that He might ask them to put in a good word for Him with the authorities.

They also thought that Bahá'u'lláh would act just like other people; that he would call on the eminent people to ask for special privileges for Himself. That was the custom in those days. It was not quite honest, of course, but, well, nearly everyone did it. And when nearly everyone does something, people no longer think it is so bad.

Do you think that a Divine Messenger would need to do anything like that? That He would need to call on people to help Him, or to ask for special privileges for Himself, or try to keep on the right side of others? Of course not! A Messenger is far above all that. He does not need people. It is just the other way round: people need Him. So Bahá'u'lláh did not call on the eminent people to keep on the right side of them or to ask for special privileges for Himself.

Some people respected Him very highly because of this. One of these, a man who had come from Persia, even said that he was extremely proud of his countryman. He often felt ashamed of the greed of Persian princes who all had the habit of accepting as many presents as they could get. He was glad to hear of someone who did not act like that.

There were also people who had a different opinion. They were angry with Bahá'u'lláh because He visited no one. One of these was Ḥusayn Khán, the Persian ambassador in Constantinople. He was angry because Bahá'u'lláh did not pay a visit to the Persian Embassy.

The Persian authorities kept telling Ḥusayn Khán that he should say bad things about Bahá'u'lláh. And now he had the chance. He could now call Bahá'u'lláh proud and stubborn. He said that Bahá'u'lláh felt that He did not need to obey the laws of the land and that He was making plans which could endanger the government.

Ḥusayn Khán's stories were, of course, not true. For Bahá'u'lláh teaches us that we should obey the government's laws, and Bahá'u'lláh Himself always set a good example. He teaches us the Laws of God and there is no one who keeps these better than the Messenger Himself.

Ḥusayn Khán kept on telling his false stories until he finally got his way: the authorities in Constantinople gave orders for Bahá'u'lláh to leave for Adrianople. Once again Bahá'u'lláh was exiled. Once again it was in the middle of winter, just like when He and His family had been banished from Ṭihrán.

It was no way to treat people! Certainly not in such a cold winter. It was so cold that even people a hundred years old could not remember one as cold. Rivers which were usually never frozen were now covered in ice. Even animals which usually lived outdoors in other winters were frozen to death. When the exiles needed water on their journey to Adrianople, they first had to make a huge fire to melt the ice.

It was no way to treat people! They had been given no time to buy warm clothing. They had to leave in such a hurry, on open carts or the backs of mules so that they could hardly protect themselves from the cold and the wind. This terrible journey lasted for twelve days.

They were exhausted when they reached Adrianople.

The departure from Constantinople was a great humiliation. When Bahá'u'lláh had arrived there He was received as a king. Now, four months later, He was just sent away.

Bahá'u'lláh knew that there were people who wanted to humiliate Him. But He also knew that in time He would be triumphant. Just listen to what Bahá'u'lláh wrote in His letter to Ḥusayn Khán: 'Were all the governments on earth to unite and take My life and the lives of all who bear this name, this Divine Fire would never be quenched . . . Whatever may yet befall us, great shall be our gain, and manifest the loss wherewith they shall be afflicted.'

21

Bahá'u'lláh is Poisoned

The life of every Messenger of God has been difficult. They have all suffered a great deal because of what their opponents have done to Them.

Moses suffered under the Egyptian Pharaoh, Jesus under the Jews and the Báb under the leaders of Islám. Bahá'u'lláh also had powerful enemies who opposed Him, among them the Sháh of Persia and the Sultán of the Ottoman Empire.

But Bahá'u'lláh suffered the most through those who claimed that they were His followers and at the same time continually plotted against Him. In particular, Bahá'u'lláh's half-brother, Mírzá Yaḥyá, made His life terribly difficult.

Mírzá Yaḥyá was a boy of about nine when his father died. Bahá'u'lláh was then twenty-two. From that time, Bahá'u'lláh looked after Mírzá Yaḥyá as a father. Even when he was grown up, Bahá'u'lláh often took him into His protection. Even if Mírzá Yaḥyá had done something wrong, Bahá'u'lláh would ask those who knew about it not to tell anyone else. But Mírzá Yaḥyá was extremely ungrateful. No matter how well Bahá'u'lláh and His family treated him, he was never satisfied.

Mírzá Yaḥyá was also an ambitious man. He wanted the believers to turn to him as their leader. This became obvious once again in Adrianople. When Bahá'u'lláh had settled there with His family and followers, it was not long before the people became very fond of them. The people found they could trust the Bahá'ís. If they bought anything from them, they were always treated fairly. It was not long either before they were attracted to Bahá'u'lláh. Even the governor of Adrianople became one of His admirers.

Just as in Baghdád, Mírzá Yahyá again became jealous. He wanted to receive the honour which was shown to Bahá'u'lláh. Mírzá Yahyá wanted the believers to follow him and regard him as their leader. But he was no match for Bahá'u'lláh. When he was in Bahá'u'lláh's presence he was speechless. He could not utter a word, so overwhelmed was he by the majesty of Bahá'u'lláh.

One thing was clear: Mírzá Yahyá would never become the leader of the Bahá'ís by honest means. But he was determined to be the leader. If it could not be done by honest means, then it would have to be some underhand way. Mírzá Yahyá would stop at nothing. He did not even hesitate to plot to kill Bahá'u'lláh. You just can't understand it. When Mírzá Yahyá was a little boy, Bahá'u'lláh had looked after him like a father. And in spite of all the wrong which he had done, Bahá'u'lláh had always treated him well. And now Mírzá Yahyá wanted to kill his Brother.

He began to do something which he never used to do. He invited Bahá'u'lláh occasionally to tea at his house. Meanwhile he learned how to make poison. And one day when Bahá'u'lláh was visiting him, he smeared poison on Bahá'u'lláh's teacup.

The result was terrible. Bahá'u'lláh became ill – very, very ill. For a whole month He suffered a lot of pain and had a high fever. They sent for the doctor. He was

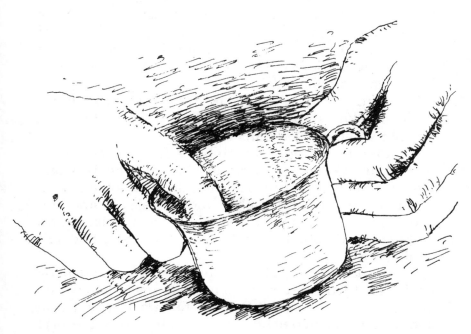

alarmed by the paleness of Bahá'u'lláh's complexion and thought that He would die. He fell at the feet of Bahá'u'lláh and then, without prescribing any medicine, he went away. A few days later the doctor became ill and died.

Bahá'u'lláh has said that this doctor sacrificed his own life for Him. And this allowed Him to get well. But He never recovered completely. After He was poisoned, His hands always shook a little. He could never again write as beautifully as He had before this happened.

Once again, Bahá'u'lláh took Mírzá Yaḥyá under His protection. He told His followers, who knew what Mírzá Yaḥyá had done, that they must tell no one.

Then what did Mírzá Yaḥyá do? He said that Bahá'u'lláh had tried to poison him! But no one believed him. The people knew that Bahá'u'lláh was a source of love and forgiveness. And because Mírzá Yaḥyá had made such a dreadful accusation, it became known that it was *he* who had poisoned Bahá'u'lláh.

Yet Mírzá Yaḥyá would not stop. His desire for leadership knew no bounds. He now began to think up another scheme to kill Bahá'u'lláh.

In those days people had no baths or showers in their houses. Instead, there were public baths. This is where they went to have a bath. They usually took some time to wash themselves thoroughly and to relax. Important people had a servant who would help them. Bahá'u'lláh's barber, Ustád, often used to look after Him and His family at the baths.

Sometimes Mírzá Yaḥyá would also be attended by Ustád. He tried for some time to make Ustád follow him and turn away from Bahá'u'lláh. But Ustád stood firm and would not listen to him; however, he showed respect to Mírzá Yaḥyá because he was the brother of Bahá'u'lláh. Then one day Mírzá Yaḥyá came to the bath and, speaking to Ustád, tried to insinuate that he should kill Bahá'u'lláh. He spoke very cleverly and very wickedly and made evil insinuations. He spoke in such a way that it appeared that *he* was the Báb's successor and that his Brother had wrongly taken over the leadership of the believers. It gradually became clear to Ustád that Mírzá Yaḥyá wanted him to kill Bahá'u'lláh.

When Ustád realised what Mírzá Yaḥyá wanted from him, he felt shattered. He felt as if the whole building had fallen on his head. Without saying a word he left. He was furious. First, he wanted to go in again and murder

Mírzá Yahyá. But he changed his mind because he knew Bahá'u'lláh would not approve. What would he say if Bahá'u'lláh asked him why he had killed Mírzá Yahyá?

Still in a rage, he returned to the baths and shouted at Mírzá Yahyá: 'Get out of here!' Trembling all over, Mírzá Yahyá went away.

Ustád was terribly upset. He could not be calmed down. First he told Mírzá Músá (Bahá'u'lláh's faithful brother), then 'Abdu'l-Bahá. Then he told the secretary, who told Bahá'u'lláh. Bahá'u'lláh said that Ustád must not speak of it to anyone.

That evening Ustád collected all the writings of Mírzá Yahyá. He took them to the house of Bahá'u'lláh to burn them. The friends said he should not do it. But Ustád said: 'Until today I had respect for Mírzá Yahyá, but now he is less than a dog in my sight.'

And Mírzá Yahyá – had he learned his lesson? Would he at last stop making trouble all the time? No! He was to cause Bahá'u'lláh more suffering.

22

The Most Great Separation

Ustád, Bahá'u'lláh's barber, was still full of what had happened. He had been ordered by Bahá'u'lláh to say nothing about it. But Ustád simply could not hold his tongue. After all, what was the situation?

Mírzá Yaḥyá wanted to kill Bahá'u'lláh. First he had tried to poison Him. Luckily Bahá'u'lláh did not die of this. Then Mírzá Yaḥyá had asked Ustád at the baths if he would assassinate Bahá'u'lláh. But he should never have asked Ustád such a thing. Ustád loved Bahá'u'lláh very much. He could never have harmed Him. He thought it terrible that Mírzá Yaḥyá should even dare to suggest such a thing to him. He just could not keep it to himself. So it was not long before the believers in Adrianople knew what had happened.

After this, Bahá'u'lláh decided to announce officially to Mírzá Yaḥyá Who He was. Bahá'u'lláh revealed a Tablet in which He said that He was the Source of Divine Revelation. He was the One the Báb had repeatedly told His followers would soon appear. Bahá'u'lláh also said that Mírzá Yaḥyá must follow Him.

Bahá'u'lláh gave this Tablet to His secretary. He was to go to Mírzá Yaḥyá with it and read the Tablet aloud to him. Then he was to wait for Mírzá Yaḥyá's answer.

Mírzá Yaḥyá asked if he could have one day's grace to think about his answer. This was granted. On the next day he gave his answer. Do you know what Mírzá Yaḥyá dared to say? He said that he himself was the receiver of a divine revelation. He even gave the day and the time at which he had received this revelation. He also said that all the peoples of the world should submit themselves to him.

This reply from Mírzá Yaḥyá could have caused disagreements among the believers. Bahá'u'lláh certainly did not want anyone to fight over Him. There was nothing He hated so much as disunity. So He decided to withdraw to a house close by. This was the house of Riḍá Big. He wanted to speak to no one. Only His family could come with Him.

This was not the first time that Bahá'u'lláh had withdrawn. He had done so in Baghdád. That time, too, it was Mírzá Yaḥyá who had made His life so difficult. Bahá'u'lláh then stayed for two years in the wilderness of Sulaymáníyyih. No one in His family knew where He was. The believers were very upset because they could no longer go to see Bahá'u'lláh.

Now it was the same. The faithful followers were very sad. They could no longer listen to their Beloved telling them about God and they could no longer ask His advice. One of them later wrote: 'We were completely downcast and were very much afraid that we would be deprived forever of His presence.'

Before Bahá'u'lláh moved to the house of Riḍá Big, He ordered that His possessions be divided in two. Of everything which was in the house, furniture, bedclothes, clothing – whatever there was – half of it went to Mírzá Yaḥyá. He would also receive his full share of the money which the exiles received from the government. He and his family would get all they were entitled to. No, Mírzá Yaḥyá had no reason to complain. As usual, Bahá'u'lláh treated him very well.

And yet, as so often, Mírzá Yaḥyá was not satisfied. He went to the authorities himself to complain that he was not getting enough. He even sent one of his wives to the governor of Adrianople. She was to tell him that they were getting nothing and that the children were almost dying of hunger.

And do you know what was the worst of all? The things Mírzá Yaḥyá said were spread far and wide. And many people believed them. They even heard about it in Constantinople. There were people there who had great respect for Bahá'u'lláh and His noble and dignified behaviour. Even these people heard these bad reports. In this way Bahá'u'lláh's admirers became people who insulted and despised Him. And all because of Mírzá Yaḥyá's wicked lies.

For two whole months the believers were separated from their Beloved. For two whole months they could not see Him. They were like plants on which the sun no longer shone and, because of that, could not grow.

It was a difficult time for them. A time in which they were tested. They could choose: Shall I remain faithful to Bahá'u'lláh or shall I follow Mírzá Yaḥyá? Now it would be obvious who were the true believers.

Up to that time it had always been possible for those who were trying to destroy the Faith to mix freely with the faithful followers. In spite of all the wrong they did, they were still counted as followers. How often had they thrown the true believers into confusion? How often had they tried to lead other people astray? Very often!

Now it was plain which followers remained faithful to Bahá'u'lláh. Fortunately, in Adrianople, nearly everyone did. Only a handful went to the aid of Mírzá Yaḥyá in his wicked deeds. These were now separated from the believers. They were like dead branches which had been sawn off the living tree. It was the time of the Most Great Separation.

23

Ashraf's Mother

When the Bábís heard that Bahá'u'lláh had announced in the Garden of Riḍván that He was the Messenger of God, many of them had only one wish: they wanted to go to Him; they wanted to be with Him, to hear His words. They were quite willing to make a long and difficult pilgrimage from Persia to Adrianople, for travelling was anything but easy in those days.

One of them was Siyyid Ashraf from Zanján. Ashraf and his mother were loyal followers of the Báb. When they heard that Bahá'u'lláh had declared that He was the new Messenger, they believed in Him and were very happy. Ashraf was at that time a boy of about seventeen, but yet he made the long journey to Adrianople. He wanted to be with Bahá'u'lláh himself!

When he got back to Persia it was not long before he set out again for Adrianople. This time, one of his sisters went with him.

His mother remained behind alone in Zanján. This was very difficult for her. The people of Zanján had not seen Ashraf and his sister for a long time. 'Where could they be?' they wondered. Ashraf's uncles, in particular, were wondering where they could be. They did not want Ashraf and his sister to become Bahá'ís. Ashraf's father had already been killed earlier when the Bábís were being persecuted and they did not want the same thing to happen to Ashraf.

So they went to Ashraf's mother. They blamed her
because Ashraf's father had become a Bábí and had been
killed. And now she was doing the same with her
children. Now she was teaching them to be followers of
Bahá'u'lláh. They were angry with her and even said
nasty things about her daughter. Ashraf's mother was in
despair. She could bear it no longer. Weeping, she left
the room and in her heart begged Bahá'u'lláh to send her
children home again soon.

The next morning when Ashraf and his sister came
into the presence of Bahá'u'lláh, He told them that they

must return home at once. He said that on the previous evening their mother had prayed to Him to send them back. Ashraf's mother lived more than a thousand kilometres from Adrianople. And yet Bahá'u'lláh knew what she had begged of Him the night before. He had heard her prayer and Ashraf and his sister would depart for home as soon as possible.

On the way home it became clear how much Ashraf had changed as a result of his visit to Bahá'u'lláh. His love for Him had grown much greater than it was already. Bahá'u'lláh had given Ashraf the mission of bringing His Message to the faithful followers of the Báb. And this is what he did, with great energy and enthusiasm. His home became a centre of Bahá'í activities. Many Bábís learned from Ashraf that Bahá'u'lláh was the Promised One the Báb had said that God would soon reveal.

Ashraf had a friend who helped him a lot in his work for Bahá'u'lláh. This was Abá-Basír. Abá-Basír was blind. He had been thrown out of his home by his family when they discovered that he had become a follower of Bahá'u'lláh. Abá-Basír was very clever. He could understand Bahá'u'lláh's Tablets better than anyone. He was also very good at explaining them to others. Bahá'u'lláh had given him the name of Basír. Basír means the one who sees.

By now, too, there were more of the Muslim clergy who wanted to prevent the Faith of Bahá'u'lláh from spreading, especially in Zanján. Twenty years before, the Bábís had been fiercely persecuted there. Almost two thousand of them had been killed then, including the fathers of Ashraf and Abá-Basír. And now the new religion was beginning to grow again. The enemies did not want this to happen. So they decided that both Ashraf and Abá-Baṣír should be killed. That would put an end to the spread of the Faith. The two men were seized and thrown into prison.

First the enemies began to talk to Abá-Baṣír. They told him he would not be killed if he would say he did not believe in Bahá'u'lláh. Would Abá-Baṣír do this? Of course not! He did just the opposite: he began to talk to the enemies about Bahá'u'lláh. He showed them that He was a Messenger of God. In fact they, too, ought to believe in Him. When they heard this the clergy became furious. They saw to it that Abá-Baṣír was immediately put to death.

Afterwards they went to speak with Ashraf. The enemies did their very best to persuade him to say that he did not believe in Bahá'u'lláh. They beat him black and blue. But whatever they tried, it was no good. Ashraf refused absolutely to deny Bahá'u'lláh. Yet there were some of the enemies who wanted to save his life. They liked him because he had such good qualities and was always so kind to everyone. Some of them thought it would be a pity to kill him. But the governor had given orders for his execution, unless Ashraf would say he no longer believed in Bahá'u'lláh. So they did their best to get Ashraf to deny his Faith.

But however hard they tried, Ashraf remained firm. Then they thought they would be very crafty. They fetched Ashraf's mother. If she could see how her son had been beaten and if she saw Abá-Baṣír's body, she would surely tell Ashraf to recant his faith. After all, she would be saving his life if she did. For what mother wants her son to be put to death?

How mistaken they were! They had not reckoned with

Ashraf's mother's own steadfastness in her Faith. She would never, ever deny Bahá'u'lláh, and would never want her son to do so either. She even said to Ashraf that he would no longer be her son if he rejected Bahá'u'lláh's Truth just to save his earthly life.

So this plan did not work either. They thought of another ruse. One of them went to Ashraf, whispered something in his ear and then shouted to the onlookers that Ashraf had told him he no longer was a Bahá'í. When he heard this, Ashraf immediately said it was not true. He had not recanted his Faith and he would never do so. Then the executioner stepped forward and killed Ashraf with his sword.

When Ashraf was born his father had been killed. Now Ashraf's mother had to see her son, too, being killed before her very eyes. Yet she was not angry or rebellious against God. Rather, she was thankful that Ashraf had remained faithful to Bahá'u'lláh. Bahá'u'lláh praised her courage and trust in the following words:

'On her be My blessings, and My mercy, and My praise, and My glory. I Myself shall atone for the loss of her son – a son who now dwelleth within the tabernacle of My majesty and glory, and whose face beameth with a light that envelopeth with its radiance the Maids of Heaven in their celestial chambers, and beyond them the inmates of My Paradise and the denizens of the Cities of Holiness. Were any eye to gaze on his face, he would exclaim: "Lo, this is no other than a noble angel!"'

24

Banished Once Again

Mírzá Yaḥyá would not give up. He still wanted to be the leader of the Bábís. He had tried to poison Bahá'u'lláh. He had asked Bahá'u'lláh's barber, Ustád, to kill Him. He had had faithful followers of the Báb murdered. He had told lies about Bahá'u'lláh. And he would not stop. Another thing he and his henchmen did was to write letters to the Bábís in Persia. What kind of things did he write to them? Mírzá Yaḥyá wrote that the Bábís must follow him and obey him; he was their leader and not Bahá'u'lláh.

Many Bábís became confused as a result. One of these was Mír Muḥammad of S̲h̲íráz. He just did not know what to think. So he made the long journey to Adrianople. There he talked to the followers of Bahá'u'lláh and also to the followers of Mírzá Yaḥyá, to find out the truth for himself.

Then Mír Muḥammad heard something which he felt was very important. One of Mírzá Yaḥyá's followers told him that Mírzá Yaḥyá was willing to have a confrontation with Bahá'u'lláh in front of the people. They would then ask each other questions. The answers they would give would be sufficient for everyone listening to judge who was speaking the truth and who was not. This seemed a good idea to Mír Muḥammad. He encouraged Mírzá Yaḥyá's helper to propose this to Mírzá Yaḥyá. Then Mír Muḥammad would ask Bahá'u'lláh.

Mírzá Yaḥyá and his helpers thought that Bahá'u'lláh would never agree to such a meeting. After all, He no longer left His house very often and never went to visit Mírzá Yaḥyá at all. Well, they were mistaken. As soon as Bahá'u'lláh heard of the arrangement, He went to the mosque suggested by Mírzá Yaḥyá. When He got there, he told Mír Muḥammad to go and fetch Mírzá Yaḥyá.

Did Mírzá Yaḥyá come with Mír Muḥammad? Did he dare? Bahá'u'lláh waited for him until the sun had almost set. Many people came and went . . . but not Mírzá Yaḥyá!

The news spread like wildfire through Adrianople. Many people had come out of their homes. They wanted to see what would happen. And now they all saw what had happened. Mírzá Yaḥyá had often said that he would like to confront Bahá'u'lláh. Now he had the chance and he was missing. He was afraid. Once again it was clear that Mírzá Yaḥyá could never be a leader and that in fact he was a liar. It was now plain to the people of Adrianople Who the true leader was and who was not.

Mírzá Yaḥyá was like a big black cloud in front of the sun. You can't see the sun through a cloud like that or feel its warm rays. But of course it is shining. The sun is always shining, even behind dark clouds. A Messenger of God is like the sun. He spreads the Light of God. He always thinks about God. He can always reveal God's Word. Even when people make it very difficult for Him and He has great misfortunes, the light of the Divine Messenger still keeps shining.

Even though Mírzá Yaḥyá made things very difficult for Bahá'u'lláh, he could not stop Bahá'u'lláh's work. For during those same years in Adrianople, when Mírzá Yaḥyá unceasingly opposed Bahá'u'lláh, Bahá'u'lláh's light shone more radiantly than it ever had before.

Day and night, Bahá'u'lláh revealed Tablets in which He unfolded divine wisdom for mankind. Sometimes more than a thousand verses would be revealed in one single hour. 'Abdu'l-Bahá and several secretaries were busy for whole days and nights, writing down the verses which had been revealed. But it was impossible to keep up with it all.

It was also just at that difficult time in Adrianople that Bahá'u'lláh revealed one of His most important Tablets. This was the Tablet to the Kings. In Persian it is called the *Súriy-i-Mulúk*. Bahá'u'lláh also began to announce His station to the rulers of the world and to the leaders of religion. This was a very important event.

Other things happened in Adrianople which showed that Bahá'u'lláh's work was not to be stopped. The work of a Messenger of God is the work of God. Was there ever anyone in the world who could stop that? The citizens of Adrianople were drawn to Bahá'u'lláh as by a magnet. They became very fond of Him. If ever they found out He was out of doors, they would hurry out of their houses to go to Him. Many would fall on the ground and kiss His feet. Even the leaders of the city had great respect for Bahá'u'lláh. They regularly went to visit Him to show Him this respect.

There was something else by which you could see that Bahá'u'lláh's light could not be put out: the first pilgrims from Persia came to Adrianople. Adrianople was a very long way from Persia and the pilgrims had to make a long and dangerous journey. Yet they came.

The enemies of the Faith had exiled Bahá'u'lláh to a place far distant from the land of His birth. They thought that this would put an end to the new Faith. But what happened? Instead of coming to an end, it began to grow in Adrianople too. Even the authorities of the city became admirers of Bahá'u'lláh. His followers from Persia came to visit Him. The government ministers in Constantinople did their very best to stop the growth of the Faith. But the number of its followers just kept on increasing.

There was also a person who was plotting against Bahá'u'lláh. This was Mírzá Yahyá. He had still become no wiser. He and his helpers began to write wicked letters about Bahá'u'lláh, even to the ministers in Constantinople. They wrote that Bahá'u'lláh was intending to overthrow Constantinople with an army, that some commanders from the Bulgarian army and several thousand of His followers were going to assist Him.

It was all lies. Yet the government became alarmed at all these reports. The ministers took them to Sultán 'Abdu'l-'Azíz and he gave orders that Bahá'u'lláh and His followers were to leave Adrianople. Bahá'u'lláh was exiled to the prison of 'Akká. The Sultán decreed that Mírzá Yahyá must also leave. He was banished to Cyprus, an island in the Mediterranean Sea.

Shortly afterwards, one morning quite unexpectedly Bahá'u'lláh's house was surrounded by soldiers. No one was allowed out and no one was allowed in. What was in store for Bahá'u'lláh now?

25

Leaving Adrianople

Just imagine that you and your family have been living for years in a nice house. You like living there. You have your friends and playmates in the neighbourhood, you know the people living near you and they know you. You know your way about, you have places where you play with other children or where you can be on your own if you want to.

Then the news suddenly comes that you have to leave your home. You and your family have to go and live somewhere else because there are those who have gossiped about you and said wicked things which are not true at all. You must leave the house as soon as possible and go to a place which you already know is horrible. It would be awful, if that happened, wouldn't it? Well, that is what happened to Bahá'u'lláh when He was living in Adrianople. Suddenly the news came that He had to leave as soon as possible and go to the prison of 'Akká.

This was now the fourth time that Bahá'u'lláh and His family had been exiled. Do you remember the previous times? The first was when He was banished from Ṭihrán. He was very ill at the time, having just been released from the dreadful prison of the Síyáh-Chál. In freezing winter weather and deep snow He and His family, with two of His brothers, made the journey to Baghdád. When they had been living there for ten years they were exiled again. They had to make a long journey to Constantinople. And when they had been there for four months the news came that they must leave. They had to depart for Adrianople as quickly as possible in the midst of a very hard winter. They were not even given time to buy warm clothing. Shivering with the cold, they arrived in Adrianople at the end of a terrible journey.

Bahá'u'lláh had now been living in Adrianople for five years. He had arrived as a prisoner. But very soon the people of Adrianople noticed that He was a very unusual person. They began to respect Him greatly and to love Him. Even the Governor of the city became one of His admirers. He tried to protect Bahá'u'lláh against the wicked lies of the authorities in Constantinople. But the enemies of the Faith kept on making trouble until finally Sulṭán 'Abdu'l-'Azíz sent orders for Bahá'u'lláh to depart.

Soon afterwards, Bahá'u'lláh's house was suddenly surrounded one morning by soldiers. No one was allowed to enter and no one could leave. This was a terrible day for the followers of Bahá'u'lláh. Many of them were arrested and put in prison. They had no idea what might happen to them. Perhaps they might even be killed. Perhaps they would be kept away from Bahá'u'lláh and taken to some place where they could no longer see Him. To them, this would be worse: not to be with Bahá'u'lláh any more. Bahá'u'lláh had even warned them that if they stayed close to Him they might get into trouble. But they wanted to stay with Him, no matter how far away He was going.

Do you know what upset His followers the most? That they did not know what might happen to Bahá'u'lláh. They wondered what the government was going to do to Him and whether the persecution would ever stop. The enemies of the Faith were continually making trouble for Him.

When the Bahá'ís had been in prison for a day and a night, they were told that they must leave Adrianople as quickly as possible. They were not even given enough time to sell their tables, chairs and lots of other things they could not bring with them. They had to do it in such haste that they got much too little money for them. Then they set out. They did not even know where they were going. Perhaps they would never see Bahá'u'lláh again. That was a terrible thought.

Do you remember what it was like when Bahá'u'lláh departed from Baghdád? The whole of Baghdád came out on the street. How sad the people were that He was leaving!

Well, it was the same in Adrianople. Crowds of people stood in front of their houses to see Him for the last time. They were filled with sorrow. And they said to each other: 'Why should He and His family be the victims of such cruel treatment? They were always kind and honest with everyone. They surely have not deserved this.'

The people's sorrow could be seen on their faces. They came close to Bahá'u'lláh to kiss His hands. Others knelt on the ground to touch His clothing and kiss the hem of His cloak. It was as if the very walls and gates of the city were sorrowing.

And so Bahá'u'lláh departed from Adrianople.

26

Sulṭán ʻAbduʼl-ʻAzíz

Sulṭán ʻAbduʼl-ʻAzíz was a powerful man. He was the ruler of the huge Ottoman Empire. Millions of people were his subjects and had to obey him. He was very rich and possessed splendid palaces with large, beautiful gardens in Constantinople. Sulṭán ʻAbduʼl-ʻAzíz ruled over millions of people. But did he take good care of them? Did he see that the poor had enough to eat or enough clothes to wear? Did his government see that the children could go to school? Did he see that the people in his kingdom were justly treated? And what about people in prison, how did they fare?

Well, we have seen how Baháʼuʼlláh was treated. He had done nothing wrong. Yet the Sulṭán had had a hand in forcing Him and His family to move from Baghdád to Constantinople. And shortly afterwards, in the middle of a hard winter, they had to leave for Adrianople. This was also on the orders of Sulṭán ʻAbduʼl-ʻAzíz.

Now Baháʼuʼlláh was on another journey. Sulṭán ʻAbduʼl-ʻAzíz had decreed that Baháʼuʼlláh should go to the prison of ʻAkká. This was a terrible prospect. Everyone knew that only the worst criminals were sent to that prison.

The first part of the journey was overland, to the port of Gallipoli. From there they would continue by sea. As they travelled to Gallipoli, soldiers accompanied Baháʼuʼlláh. In Gallipoli, their captain came to say goodbye to Baháʼuʼlláh. He was extremely humble and

polite. He told Bahá'u'lláh that he was sorry to see Him treated like this by the authorities. Bahá'u'lláh then said to him: 'Tell the king that this territory will pass out of his hands, and his affairs will be thrown into confusion. Not I speak these words, but God speaketh them.'

Bahá'u'lláh said other things to the captain, too. He said that the Sultán should have seen to it that a meeting was held and should have invited Bahá'u'lláh to that meeting. Then the Sultán should himself have investigated Bahá'u'lláh's case. He should have found out for himself whether Bahá'u'lláh had done anything which was against the Will of God. He should have asked Bahá'u'lláh to prove the truth of His words. If the Sultán had found Bahá'u'lláh to be wanting, then he could have done what he liked with Him. But what the Sultán was doing now was wrong. He should never have allowed so much hostility and injustice. There was no reason whatever for it. The Sultán was just doing what wicked people had told him to do.

The captain listened very attentively to Bahá'u'lláh and promised Him that he would take His message to the Sultán. But would it do any good? Would it change Sultán 'Abdu'l-'Azíz? Would he rule his enormous kingdom any better afterwards?

Bahá'u'lláh had already warned Sultán 'Abdu'l-'Azíz. He was actually the first king to whom Bahá'u'lláh announced that He was the Messenger of God for this Age. He had already written to him saying he must look after his country better; that he must not leave his work to ministers who were not doing what was good for the country and its people but often did what was of advantage to themselves. It was a strange situation: the king listened to the ministers instead of the other way round. If only they had been honest and wise ministers! But they certainly were neither!

Did Sulṭán 'Abdu'l-'Azíz listen to Bahá'u'lláh's warnings? No, alas, he did not. Bahá'u'lláh prophesied that his territory would be taken from him. This is what happened. The Sulṭán came to a very bad end.

Within ten years, Sulṭán 'Abdu'l-'Azíz was deposed from his throne. The people no longer wanted him for their king. He could not govern and had spent far too much money on his own pleasures. There was no one left to help him. Four days later he was assassinated.

His huge kingdom came to a bad end too. One year after Sulṭán 'Abdu'l-'Azíz had been killed a dreadful war broke out between the Ottoman Empire and Russia. The Russian armies conquered a large piece of Ottoman territory. In this war, tens of thousands of people died of starvation and disease. The people suffered terribly.

After that, more wars came. At last there was only a small piece left of the Ottoman Empire which had once been so powerful. What is left of it is now called Turkey.

Sulṭán 'Abdu'l-'Azíz was once a powerful ruler who thought he was the most important man in the world and that Bahá'u'lláh was the least important! But now hardly anyone remembers Sulṭán 'Abdu'l-'Azíz. No one remembers the king who would not listen to the advice of Bahá'u'lláh.

27

The Meeting

Everything had turned out for the best! The believers were allowed to go with Bahá'u'lláh to 'Akká. In Gallipoli they all boarded the ship together. But how anxious they had been!

Up to the time they went on board, the Bahá'ís from Adrianople had not known what would happen to them. Nor did they know where Bahá'u'lláh was being sent, or whether they could go with Him. They had all hoped they would be going to the same place as Bahá'u'lláh.

At first they heard that the authorities had decided to send Bahá'u'lláh and two of His brothers and a servant to the prison city of 'Akká and that all the others would go to Constantinople. They were very sad. Now they would be separated from Him. But finally the authorities decided that all could be sent together to 'Akká. Some of the believers had to pay their own fares. This they were only too glad to do. At least it meant that they could stay with Bahá'u'lláh!

To be able to stay with Bahá'u'lláh – they would do anything for this. For this they would even go to prison. Bahá'u'lláh had warned them that things would get more difficult for them than ever. Anyone who did not feel strong enough to bear great difficulties would be better off not coming with Him but going somewhere else. There was still time to change their minds; once they were on board it would be too late.

But none of His followers would leave Him. Everyone went with Him. Because however hard their lives were, the worst of all was to be separated from Him.

The inhabitants of Gallipoli could not understand it. There was a Prisoner Who had to go to the prison of 'Akká. That was where only the worst criminals were sent. And those people with Him wanted to go there too! They were even willing to pay their own fares. What kind of people were they to go willingly with someone into prison and to pay their own fares into the bargain? But then, *they* did not know Who Bahá'u'lláh was!

The ship arrived in Alexandria about four days later. Alexandria is a port in Egypt. Here they had to change over to another ship. Fortunately it was not leaving straight away. Now they had time to buy some food and drink in the city. Some of them were allowed to land to do their shopping.

One of these was Muḥammad Ibráhím. He was walking down the street when suddenly he heard someone call his name. He stopped in amazement and looked around him. How could this be? How could anyone in this strange city be calling his name? Then he saw that he was being called from the prison nearby.

Ah! A familiar face. It was Nabíl, one of the most faithful followers of Bahá'u'lláh!

Nabíl had been sent by Bahá'u'lláh to Egypt. Some of the friends had been treated badly there and Nabíl had had to go to their aid. And now he was in prison in Alexandria. What a coincidence!

Muḥammad Ibráhím at once told Nabíl what had happened: Bahá'u'lláh had been exiled from Adrianople to 'Akká. With His followers He was now travelling by steamer to 'Akká. The ship was in the dock here and a few people were allowed off to buy things. Muḥammad Ibráhím could not say very much because the soldiers who had accompanied him to watch him told him they must now move on.

Alone and despairing, Nabíl remained behind in his prison cell. Now he was so close to Bahá'u'lláh and yet he could not go to Him. What could he do?

That evening Fáris Effendi entered Nabíl's cell. Fáris was a doctor. The two men had become very good friends in prison. Nabíl had told Fáris about Bahá'u'lláh. And Fáris had then become a Bahá'í.

When Fáris heard that his friend was so upset, he became almost more upset himself. What could they do? Fortunately, Fáris had an idea. He said: 'We will not get permission to visit the ship. But we can still do something. You write whatever message you like. And I will write something too. Tomorrow some of my friends are coming here. We'll give them the letters to take to the ship.'

Then they each wrote a letter to Bahá'u'lláh.

Next morning Constantine the watchmaker came to the prison. They gave their letters to him to take to the ship. From the roof of the prison they could see the harbour. So they could see quite well the ship on which Bahá'u'lláh was.

What a calamity! The ship was setting sail. First it stopped for about fifteen minutes. Then it sailed out of the harbour. Nabíl and Fáris were then almost certain that their plan had failed.

But they were wrong! Constantine had taken a small boat and followed the ship. When the ship carrying Bahá'u'lláh had sailed away, Constantine did not give up. He kept on going! The ship's captain saw the small

100

boat trying to catch up with them. And then something happened which no one expected. The captain ordered the ship to stop. The passengers on board were astonished that the captain would stop the ship for this reason. Then they saw Constantine climb up the rope ladder onto the deck and go to where Bahá'u'lláh and His followers were to be found. So the letters reached Bahá'u'lláh after all.

In the prison, the doctor and Nabíl waited anxiously. With tears in their eyes, they had seen the ship carrying their Beloved depart. He was gone to the prison city of 'Akká. He had been so near and yet they had not been able to see Him.

Suddenly Constantine arrived and called out: 'By God, I have seen the Father of Christ Himself!'

How happy Nabíl and Fáris were then! Bahá'u'lláh had received their letters after all. On the ship, Bahá'u'lláh had revealed a Tablet for them. 'Abdu'l-Bahá had hastily written a letter too and Mírzá Mihdí, one of Bahá'u'lláh's other sons, had wrapped a handful of sweets in a piece of paper and given it to Constantine.

Now they were no longer sorrowful. Just imagine. They had both received a letter from Bahá'u'lláh. Their hearts were filled to overflowing with happiness.

28

Arrival in 'Akká

Nineteen days earlier, Bahá'u'lláh had left Adrianople. It had been a difficult journey. For ten days He had been on board a steamer, confined in a place which was much too small for Bahá'u'lláh and the seventy people who had sailed with Him. And yet their troubles were not yet over. Not by any means. They were about to get worse.

It all started when the ship arrived in Haifa. Four faithful followers were separated from Him. They had to go with Mírzá Yaḥyá to the island of Cyprus in the Mediterranean Sea. These were the orders of Sulṭán 'Abdu'l-'Azíz. But they would much rather have stayed with Bahá'u'lláh and did not want to go with Mírzá Yaḥyá at all. 'Abdu'l-Ghaffár was one of these. The moment that Bahá'u'lláh disembarked from the steamship, 'Abdu'l-Ghaffár shouted loudly: 'Yá Bahá'u'l-Abhá!' and jumped off the ship into the sea. If he could not stay with Bahá'u'lláh, then he would rather drown himself. And this is what he almost did. They dragged him from the water just in time. But 'Abdu'l-Ghaffár still had to go to Cyprus. The Sulṭán's orders had to be carried out.

Bahá'u'lláh and His family and the followers who were allowed to accompany Him were transferred to a small sailing boat which was to take them from Haifa to 'Akká. It is not a long way. When you are in Haifa you can see 'Akká on the other side of the bay. And yet the journey took a long time, almost the whole day. There was very little wind to fill the sails and they hardly moved at all. It was also terribly hot that day. The sun burned down on their heads all the time. On the boat there was no shade at all to be found.

Many of the inhabitants of 'Akká stood watching curiously when Bahá'u'lláh arrived. They wanted to see the 'God of the Persians'. This is what they called Bahá'u'lláh. It was not nice to see so many inquisitive people. They shouted ugly things at Bahá'u'lláh and His companions. Sometimes they cursed and swore so badly that the Bahá'ís were afraid.

The poor folk of 'Akká knew no better. It was only to be expected. In the mosques of 'Akká they had been told that Bahá'u'lláh and His followers were unbelievers, criminals who wanted to destroy the religion of God. The inhabitants of 'Akká had been warned not to speak to these prisoners.

'Akká was an ugly city. Once it had been famous. But when Bahá'u'lláh arrived, not much of its former glory was left. It had become a prison city to which the worst criminals were sent. It was also a dirty city, with filthy streets and lots of vermin. They did not even have clean drinking water and the smell was dreadful. The people used to say sometimes as a joke that if birds flew over 'Akká, they would fall down dead from the stench. That's how bad it was!

So Bahá'u'lláh arrived in 'Akká as a Prisoner. He and His family and followers had had a long, difficult journey. They were tired, hungry and thirsty. But the first night they got nothing to eat. When they asked if they could have some water, they did not even get that – just imagine, after such a burning hot day. They had no beds either. They had to sleep on the floor.

It was the Plan of God that Bahá'u'lláh should come to 'Akká. God wanted Bahá'u'lláh to come to the Holy Land. More than two thousand years ago the prophets of Israel had foretold it.

No one can say that Bahá'u'lláh travelled to the Holy Land of His own accord. It was in fact the opponents of the Faith who made it happen. They had sent Him from place to place. He had been exiled three times already: first to Baghdád and from there to Constantinople; shortly afterwards all the way to Adrianople. His enemies thought then: now He is so far away, we'll never hear anything more about Him. But they were wrong. Finally they sent Him to the infamous prison of 'Akká. They thought they had got rid of Him at last. They thought they could destroy the new religion.

How wrong they were! Instead of stopping the progress of the Faith, they had helped it. The enemies of the Faith had done exactly what was needed to fulfil the Plan of God.

29

The Most Great Prison

In Adrianople Bahá'u'lláh had warned the Bahá'ís: anyone who came with Him must be prepared for hardship. Whoever thought they could not bear it should go somewhere else while they still had the chance. But no one went. They all wanted to stay with Bahá'u'lláh, no matter to what place He might be banished.

It was a terrible hardship to be in prison in 'Akká. Their troubles began the very first evening. Bahá'u'lláh and His family and followers were tired, hungry and, above all, thirsty. They had spent nearly all day in the burning sun on the sailing ship. They asked the prison guards if they could have some water. But they got none. They got no food either and they had no beds to sleep on. They had to sleep on the hard floor. Hardly anyone could sleep the first night.

Next day they were given bread. Black, salty bread; you would have to be very hungry to eat it, it tasted so awful. They could also get water from a well near the prison. But that was dirty, it smelled bad and was undrinkable.

Do you know what happens if people are living in a place which is dirty and full of disease, if they do not get good food and have no clean drinking water? They get sick. So it was not long before nearly all the Bahá'ís fell ill. They had a high fever and no bedding on which to lie

comfortably to get well. Only 'Abdu'l-Bahá and one or two others did not get ill. They were kept going night and day looking after the sick friends.

Three of Bahá'u'lláh's followers died, two of them on the same night. The Bahá'ís asked their guards if they could bury their friends somewhere outside the prison. They wanted to do this themselves. Then at least they would be sure that their friends would have a proper burial in the way Bahá'u'lláh had taught them.

But no one was allowed out of the prison. The guards said that they must give them money and that they would take care of the funeral. Where were they to get the money? Bahá'u'lláh gave the rug on which He slept to the guards to be sold, so that with the money the guards could arrange a proper burial. It was worth at least twice as much as they needed. And yet the guards sold the rug and kept the money for themselves. They dug a hole somewhere and threw in the bodies, still wearing the clothes in which they had died, unwashed and without coffins.

The guards were rough, cruel men. They were often very unkind to the Bahá'ís. But no matter what they did or how unkind they were, the Bahá'ís kept their patience. They were never angry in return. This surprised the guards. They had been used to prisoners who shouted things back at them and behaved in a hostile way.

These people, the Bahá'ís, were always polite. They never tried to get their own back. This had a great influence on the guards. They began to change. How could they keep on being so unkind to people who never were nasty to them? After a while the guards began to treat the Bahá'ís better and were not so harsh towards them.

There was something else which made life in the prison very hard. Sulṭán 'Abdu'l-'Azíz and his ministers had decided that the Bahá'ís were to have contact with no one. They were never allowed any visitors. They were never allowed to visit anyone. They even gave orders that Bahá'u'lláh should not be allowed to talk to His followers. Only His family were allowed to be with Him, no one else.

This was very hard for the pilgrims too. The moment they heard that Bahá'u'lláh was in prison in 'Akká, some of them set out to travel there. They had a long, difficult journey over high mountains and scorching deserts. But to be with Bahá'u'lláh for a few days would be worth it all. But what a disaster! When at long last they arrived in 'Akká they could not see Him. As soon as the police found out that they were Bahá'ís who wanted to visit Bahá'u'lláh, they were thrown out of the city. Poor pilgrims! There was only one thing left to do.

Around 'Akká were high walls. It had once been a fortified city; the soldiers could defend it better from behind high walls. The pilgrims used to stand beyond the second moat which surrounded the city and turn towards the Prison so that they could see the window behind which Bahá'u'lláh was imprisoned. Then they would wait, full of expectation. Would they see Bahá'u'lláh?

How happy they were if they saw Him appear behind the bars. And how happy they were if He waved to them from behind the bars. They had only glimpsed Bahá'u'lláh from a distance, yet most of them travelled back home with thankful hearts. They thought again and again of that one moment when they had seen Bahá'u'lláh and He had waved to them. It was the most wonderful moment of their lives.

Life in the prison in 'Akká was terribly difficult for Bahá'u'lláh. You remember that Bahá'u'lláh had once before been thrown into a prison? That was in Ṭihrán, in a dark dungeon, deep underground. It was called the Síyáh-Chál. It was cold and dirty there and the smell was dreadful. Bahá'u'lláh's feet were kept in stocks and He had a chain weighing fifty kilos round His neck.

Yet Bahá'u'lláh's sufferings in the prison of 'Akká were even greater. That is why He called this prison the 'Most Great Prison'. We should not forget this name.

30

Badí'

'Have you no son old enough to help you?' asked Nabíl when he saw that the old man with whom he was staying had to do everything himself.

'Yes, I have but he will not obey me. He never does what I tell him. He's a troublesome boy and he breaks my heart,' said the old man.

'Bring him to me some time. I would like to see him,' said Nabíl.

This was done. When he entered, Nabíl saw that the son was a tall, lanky boy with a simple heart. His name was Áqá Buzurg. Nabíl asked the father to let Áqá Buzurg look after him as long as he was staying in the house.

When they were together, Nabíl began to tell Áqá Buzurg about Bahá'u'lláh. He read aloud a poem to him which Bahá'u'lláh had written when He was in the wilderness of Sulaymáníyyih. In this poem Bahá'u'lláh describes His sufferings and His troubles. Áqá Buzurg's cheeks became red when he heard these divine verses. Tears sprang to his eyes. He began to weep loudly. He began to regret the bad life he had been leading. He became attracted to the words of Bahá'u'lláh. At night neither of them could sleep. So together they read the holy writings until the dawn came. In a short time, the words of Bahá'u'lláh had changed Áqá Buzurg completely.

Áqá Buzurg asked his father if he could go with Nabíl when he travelled on around Persia.

'Not now,' replied his father. 'First you must learn to read and write and study the *Book of Certitude* with your teacher. Then you must copy out the *Book of Certitude*. When you've done all that, you can go travelling.'

A few months later Áqá Buzurg was ready to depart. He first went to Baghdád to help the Bahá'ís there. He became their water-carrier. He also fetched water for the flowers in the garden of the house where Bahá'u'lláh had lived. In those days people had no taps in their houses. If they needed water, they had to go to the well or a river, so someone who helped to fetch the water was very useful.

It was not long before Áqá Buzurg wanted to go travelling again. Now he wanted to go to 'Akká, to Bahá'u'lláh. He longed to be with Bahá'u'lláh. So he made the long, difficult journey to 'Akká on foot. And it was a very long way!

Áqá Buzurg knew he had to be careful if he wanted to get into 'Akká. If the police found out he was a Bahá'í he would be sent away at once. This must not happen, not after such a long journey. He kept his ordinary clothes on, the clothes of a water-carrier. And this way he was able to walk into 'Akká unnoticed.

But now came the hardest bit. No one was allowed to visit Bahá'u'lláh in the prison, no one at all. If Áqá Buzurg went to the prison and asked to see Bahá'u'lláh, what would happen? He would be sent away from 'Akká immediately. If that happened, he would never get back into the city again. Then he would be even further from his goal. But what could he do? How could he get to see Bahá'u'lláh? Áqá Buzurg was getting desperate.

There was one thing he could do. He went to the mosque to pray. Would this solve his problem?

In the evening a little group of Persians came into the mosque. To his great relief, Áqá Buzurg saw that one of these was 'Abdu'l-Bahá. Áqá Buzurg recognised Him at once. Quickly, he wrote a note and pressed it into 'Abdu'l-Bahá's hand, very cautiously, so that no one would see, or else his plan might fail at the last moment.

Áqá Buzurg's prayers were heard! That very evening 'Abdu'l-Bahá arranged for him to come to see Bahá'u'lláh in the prison. However hard it had been, Áqá Buzurg had still reached his goal.

Bahá'u'lláh knew that Áqá Buzurg was coming. He had a very important task for him to do.

Bahá'u'lláh, while He was still living in Adrianople, had written letters to many of the Kings and Rulers of the world. All these letters had been delivered – except one. That special letter was to the Sháh of Persia. It could not be sent in the ordinary way because the Sháh's servants were not to be trusted. If his servants thought that he should not read any letter, they would tear it up or burn it, and it might well be that the Sháh would never receive the letter. So the letter from Bahá'u'lláh had to be handed personally to the Sháh by someone whom Bahá'u'lláh would trust absolutely to see that the letter reached its destination. This person was Áqá Buzurg.

Twice, Áqá Buzurg visited Bahá'u'lláh in the Most Great Prison. These visits to Bahá'u'lláh changed him even more than he had changed already. The change was so great that Bahá'u'lláh gave him a new name: Badí', which means 'Wonderful'.

During these visits Bahá'u'lláh spoke to Badí' about the Letter which must be taken to the Sháh. It was a dangerous mission. The bearer of the letter might well be killed. Badí' knew this only too well. Yet he asked if he could do it.

115

Many others had asked Bahá'u'lláh before if they could take the letter to the Sháh but He had never agreed. Now Badí' asked Him and He gave permission to Badí' to do so. Bahá'u'lláh knew that this seventeen-year-old boy could carry out this difficult and dangerous mission.

31

Badí' Goes to the Sháh

Badí' knew how dangerous his mission was. Perhaps he would be killed. Yet he wanted to do it. He had asked if he might be allowed to take the Letter from Bahá'u'lláh to the Sháh. First he had made the journey to 'Akká to be with Bahá'u'lláh. Now he was going back to Persia, a journey which was over a hundred days' walk.

Badí' was in a hurry. He wanted to get the Letter to the Sháh as soon as possible. As soon as he had the Letter, he set out. He was told that he should wait to receive money for his journey. But when a messenger from Bahá'u'lláh came to bring him the money, Badí' had already left. He was on his way to Persia, bearing Bahá'u'lláh's Letter to the Sháh.

Badí' travelled alone, all alone. This Bahá'u'lláh had told him he must do. Nor was he to visit any Bahá'ís on the way. Badí' told no one the purpose of his journey. Everyone just thought he was on his way home.

Bahá'u'lláh had given Badí' another instruction. He was to deliver the Letter to the Sháh himself. No one else was to do it for him. Then he would at least be certain that the Sháh himself had received the Letter and that it had not been torn up by his servants or hidden away.

How did Badí' make this long journey from 'Akká to Persia on foot, over high mountains and through scorching deserts? We know from someone who saw Badí' on his journey that he looked very happy and was very cheerful. It was as if he were going to a party. Every time he had walked some distance he stopped, got off the road, stood facing 'Akká and bowed his forehead to the ground. What did he do then, do you think? He began to pray. He prayed to God that he would not be deprived of his mission and asked God to give him strength to fulfil it.

After travelling for four months, Badí' arrived in Ṭihrán. He asked people if they knew where the Sháh was. He did not tell them why he wanted to know. That must be kept secret. They told him that the Sháh was at one of his summer palaces. So that is where Badí' went.

How could he ensure that the Sháh received the Letter? Bahá'u'lláh had written that no one but he was to hand it to the Sháh. He could not go into the palace and say he had a letter which he must hand to the Sháh himself. They would never allow him to see the Sháh.

Badí' went to sit on a hill beside the road along which he knew the Sháh might come. For one, two, even three days he waited. People naturally thought this was strange. 'Why is that man always sitting on that hill?' they wondered.

Badí' waited patiently until at last the Sháh came along. Calmly and with dignity, Badí' stepped forward and said to him that he had an important message for him. By the way Badí' spoke, the Sháh immediately understood that the Letter was from Bahá'u'lláh. He himself had had a hand in Bahá'u'lláh's banishment to a place very far from Persia. And now someone had suddenly appeared before him with a Letter from Bahá'u'lláh.

The Sháh took the Letter and told his servants to take Badí' prisoner. They were to ask him who his friends

were and where they could be found. At first he was to be kindly treated but if he would say nothing, they could use harsh methods to get him to talk.

The <u>Sh</u>áh's men asked Badí' all kinds of questions. First, kindly, 'From where do you bring this Letter?' 'Who gave you this Letter?' 'How long ago?' 'Who are your friends?'

Badí' told them frankly how it had happened: he had received the Letter for the <u>Sh</u>áh from Bahá'u'lláh in the prison of 'Akká. Bahá'u'lláh had warned him that it was a dangerous mission. Yet he wanted to undertake it, even when he knew that he might be killed. It was three months since he had left 'Akká. Here, he had waited for a favourable opportunity to give the Letter to the <u>Sh</u>áh. Fortunately, the chance had come. 'If you are looking for the Bahá'ís, there are a great number in Persia,' said Badí'. 'And if you want my friends: I travelled all the way on my own.'

The <u>Sh</u>áh's servants then wanted to force Badí' to tell them the names of his companions and the names of the Bahá'ís in Persia. They told him if he would tell them the names they would see that he was set free and would save him from death.

But this did not frighten Badí'. He even said he was longing for them to put him to death.

32

Badí' – Pride of the Martyrs

The <u>Sh</u>áh's men kept on trying. They kept asking Badí'
who his friends were and who had travelled with him
from 'Akká to Persia. But Badí' had travelled alone as
Bahá'u'lláh had told him to.

At first they were not unkind to him. But Badí' could
give them no names. Then they began to treat him
roughly, then more and more roughly and cruelly. They
bastinadoed him: this means that they beat the soles of
his feet with sticks or whipped them. It should have been
very painful but it was as if Badí' felt no pain; he never
moved. They even held red hot irons to his body. It was
as if this did not hurt Badí' either. He laughed when they
said they were going to do it again. The bullies could not
understand it. They had never seen anything like it
before.

For three days they tortured Badí' in this way. But no
matter what they did, Badí' said nothing. Then they
killed him. They killed him for bringing a Letter from
Bahá'u'lláh to the <u>Sh</u>áh.

What was contained in the Letter? Bahá'u'lláh told the
<u>Sh</u>áh that He had been a man like others when the breeze
of God blew over Him and gave Him the knowledge of all
things. His words were from God, not from Himself. He
asked the king to look with justice upon Him, and to pay
heed to the Word of God. If the <u>Sh</u>áh would listen to the

divine words, he would no longer think it important to be king of a great country.

What did the <u>Sh</u>áh do with the Letter he had received from Badí‘? He gave it to the clergy and told them they should answer it. But the clergy did not do what the <u>Sh</u>áh had asked them. Instead, they said that the man who had brought this Letter to the <u>Sh</u>áh should be killed.

Náṣiri’d-Dín <u>Sh</u>áh was not a ruler who looked after his country properly. During the years of his reign things got worse in Persia. There were hardly any honest officials left. They nearly always tried to make money in a dishonest way. This was often at the expense of the ordinary people who in any case earned very little. The <u>Sh</u>áh himself did not take care of his people. He was far too busy with his own importance and his own pleasure.

During the time that Náṣiri’d-Dín <u>Sh</u>áh ruled over Persia, terrible things happened in that country. The Báb was executed by firing squad in Tabríz. Thousands and thousands of followers of the Báb and Bahá’u’lláh were put to death. Bahá’u’lláh was sent away from Persia. After that the <u>Sh</u>áh had a hand in banishing Bahá’u’lláh to other places until finally He was imprisoned in ‘Akká. Náṣiri’d-Dín <u>Sh</u>áh did not look after his subjects well. He was a bad king. That is why Bahá’u’lláh has called him the ‘Prince of Oppressors’.

Náṣiri’d-Dín <u>Sh</u>áh also had Badí‘ put to death. His body had died, but his soul had gone on to a new life. Bahá’u’lláh wrote a letter to the father of Badí‘ and assured him that Badí‘ was not really dead but living on in another world.

Badí‘ sacrificed his life for Bahá’u’lláh when he was only seventeen years old. Bahá’u’lláh later called him the ‘Pride of the Martyrs’.

33

The Purest Branch

Bahá'u'lláh had now been in the Most Great Prison in 'Akká for nearly two years with His family and the followers who had come with Him from Adrianople. They were not allowed out of the prison, except for a few who sometimes went into the city to buy things. Then the guards went with them to make sure they would not escape. That was not really necessary. After all, the Bahá'ís had come with Bahá'u'lláh of their own accord! Who would dream of escaping? All they wanted was to be with Him.

Bahá'u'lláh was not allowed to have visitors either. Not even the pilgrims who had made the long journey from Persia were allowed to see Him. They were not even permitted to enter 'Akká. The only thing they could do was wave to the window of Bahá'u'lláh's prison cell from some distance outside the walls of the city.

One of the pilgrims was Ustád Ismá'íl. Although he was an old man he still travelled to 'Akká. But he was not allowed into the city either. So, like the other pilgrims, he hoped that he could still see Bahá'u'lláh, even for a moment.

But what a shame! Ustád Ismá'íl's eyesight was not as good as it had been. He stood for hours and hours, peering at the prison. But he still could not see Bahá'u'lláh waving to him from His prison cell. No matter how hard he tried, he could not see Him.

From the prison the Holy Family saw what was happening. Their eyes were filled with tears. How they longed for Ustád Ismá'íl to see Bahá'u'lláh and for the pilgrims to enter His presence. But they could do nothing.

Life was hard in the prison. There was only one spot where they could get some fresh air. That was on the flat roof of the building. There, they could walk up and down a little. They could look out over the sea and see Mount Carmel in the distance.

'Abdu'l-Bahá's younger brother, Mírzá Mihdí, was often on the roof. It was his custom to go up at evening when dusk was falling to say prayers and meditate. He would walk up and down and take care not to fall off the edge. But one evening he was so absorbed in his prayers that he forgot to look where he was going and fell through a skylight.

The noise of the fall and Mihdí's cries quickly brought others to see what had happened. Things did not look so good for him. He had fallen on a wooden crate which pierced his chest. They called a doctor but it was soon clear that Mírzá Mihdí was not going to get better.

Then Bahá'u'lláh asked Mírzá Mihdí what he himself wanted. He could have one wish. Mírzá Mihdí did not wish anything for himself. He was thinking at that moment of the pilgrims and said he wished that they would no longer be prevented from seeing their Beloved. Bahá'u'lláh answered that this would happen; God would grant his wish.

The day after the accident Mírzá Mihdí died.

His family and the believers were filled with grief. He was so young, only twenty-two. Mírzá Mihdí had always been kind to everyone. The Bahá'ís had learned so much from him. When they were together he had often read aloud to them from the Tablets which Bahá'u'lláh had revealed. He had taught them by his example to be courteous and patient and always to submit to the Will of God.

Because he had always served Him so faithfully, Bahá'u'lláh called His son the 'Purest Branch'.

When Bahá'u'lláh had come out of the Black Hole and the Sháh had ordered Him to leave Persia, Mírzá Mihdí was only four years old. He was too young to go on that dangerous journey in the hard winter weather. He was seven or eight before he was taken to Baghdád to be with his Father and mother. After that, when Bahá'u'lláh travelled to other places to which He was exiled, Mírzá Mihdí always went with Him. And so he had come with his family to the prison in 'Akká.

Mírzá Mihdí's mother, Navváb, could hardly be consoled at the death of her son. Her sorrow was so great that she fell ill. Bahá'u'lláh then went to her. He said to her that God had taken her son in order that His people could be free and that all mankind could become united and turn towards God. Navváb's heart was comforted by Bahá'u'lláh's assurance. After that she never cried again for the death of Mírzá Mihdí.

34

The Murder of Siyyid Muḥammad

Just before he died Mírzá Mihdí asked Bahá'u'lláh if his life might be a sacrifice for the pilgrims. At that time they could only wave to Bahá'u'lláh from a distance outside the wall of the prison. Mírzá Mihdí wanted them to be able to be with Bahá'u'lláh. Four months after the death of Mírzá Mihdí his wish was fulfilled and the gates of the prison were opened. Bahá'u'lláh and His family were allowed to leave the Most Great Prison and to live in other accommodation within the city walls.

Now they were out of prison, would Bahá'u'lláh's life be any easier? You would think so, but as it turned out things were not so much better.

For the first year, Bahá'u'lláh and His followers kept having to move. In one year they moved house four times. The last house they had then was also much too small. Thirteen people had to live in one room. And Bahá'u'lláh still remained a prisoner. He always had to stay in 'Akká and was not allowed to leave the city. He could never take a walk in the countryside which was what He loved so much.

The people of 'Akká were still very unfriendly to Bahá'u'lláh and His followers, too. After all, Bahá'u'lláh had been in prison. Criminals and murderers were put in that prison. So the people of 'Akká thought that everyone who had been in that prison was a criminal. And so they thought Bahá'u'lláh was one too.

Someone else was living in 'Akká as well who tried every day to make life for Bahá'u'lláh and His followers more difficult than it already was. This was Siyyid Muḥammad. Siyyid Muḥammad was one of Mírzá Yaḥyá's helpers. In Baghdád and Adrianople he and Mírzá Yaḥyá had together done a great deal to make life miserable for Bahá'u'lláh.

When Bahá'u'lláh was banished from Adrianople, Mírzá Yaḥyá and Siyyid Muḥammad were banished too. Mírzá Yaḥyá was sent on to the island of Cyprus in the Mediterranean Sea. Siyyid Muḥammad had to stay in 'Akká. There Siyyid Muḥammad continued to do what he had been doing for years. Whenever he could, he tried to work against Bahá'u'lláh and the Bahá'ís. He let no chance go by to speak ill of Bahá'u'lláh. What he said was all lies, of course, but the inhabitants of 'Akká knew no better and believed him.

Siyyid Muḥammad and his helpers lived in a room over the city gate. They could see everyone who entered the city, including the pilgrims who arrived at 'Akká after their journey from Persia. As soon as Siyyid Muḥammad or his henchmen recognised a pilgrim they told the police. They came and stopped the pilgrims and sent them back again.

Poor pilgrims! They had had a tiring journey and at the last moment everything went wrong. All the trouble was caused by Siyyid Muḥammad and his helpers. Some of the Bahá'ís wanted to give him a good chastising for this. How could they let him get away with it? But Bahá'u'lláh told them again and again to be patient and not retaliate in any way. This made Siyyid Muḥammad and his helpers even bolder, because whatever they did, the Bahá'ís would do nothing in return.

One of Siyyid Muḥammad's helpers even went so far as to interfere with the Writings of Bahá'u'lláh. He changed the Holy Scriptures in such a way that they contained dreadful things. Then they showed these to as many people as possible in 'Akká and told them that Bahá'u'lláh had written that. Naturally the inhabitants of 'Akká thought even less of Bahá'u'lláh than ever. The conduct of these men was disgraceful. Can you imagine how angry the Bahá'ís became? And yet Bahá'u'lláh had plainly said that they must not retaliate.

Seven of the Bahá'ís could bear it no longer. Would this mischief never end? Was it going to go on and on? It could not be allowed, they thought. It had to be stopped. Secretly, without saying anything to anyone, these seven Bahá'ís made a plan. The plan was to murder Siyyid Muḥammad and his helpers. They got revolvers for themselves and one afternoon they burst into Siyyid Muḥammad's house and shot him and two of his helpers dead.

The consequences were dreadful. All 'Akká was in an uproar.

'You see now?' said the people to each other. 'Those Bahá'ís are criminals and murderers after all.'

The cries and shouts of the people could be heard on every side. Armed with sticks and stones, swords and rifles, they made their way to the homes of Bahá'u'lláh and the other Bahá'ís. Every Bahá'í they met was taken and thrown into prison.

Bahá'u'lláh was asked to go to the government building. There the army commandant asked Him: 'Is it proper that some of your followers should act in such a manner?'

Bahá'u'lláh answered immediately: 'If one of your

soldiers were to commit a reprehensible act, would you be held responsible, and be punished in his place?'

At the end of the interrogation, no one made bold to answer Bahá'u'lláh. Afterwards, the Governor sent Him an apology for what had occurred.

The hatred of the people of 'Akká for the Bahá'ís was now greater than ever. They accused the Bahá'ís of being godless people. On the streets, where everyone could hear them, they called after them. Even their children could no longer go out without being insulted or having stones thrown at them.

Bahá'u'lláh had said over and over again to His followers that they must not take revenge. The more trouble Siyyid Muḥammad gave them, the more often Bahá'u'lláh repeated His commandment. Yet there were some who thought they should kill Siyyid Muḥammad and his helpers. They did not do what Bahá'u'lláh had told them. This was a cause of much sorrow to Bahá'u'lláh.

Listen to what Bahá'u'lláh Himself has said: 'My captivity can bring on Me no shame. Nay, by My life, it conferreth on Me glory. That which can make me ashamed is the conduct of such of My followers as profess to love Me, yet in fact follow the Evil One.'

35

The Most Holy Book, The *Kitáb-i-Aqdas*

If we were to put all the Writings that Bahá'u'lláh has revealed into books, we would have a long row of about a hundred books. And every Book, every Tablet and every Letter of Bahá'u'lláh is an important Writing. It contains the words of God. What could be more important than a book which God gives to mankind? And yet there is one book which Bahá'u'lláh Himself says is His most important book. He calls it the Most Holy Book. In Persian it is called the *Kitáb-i-Aqdas*.

The Most Holy Book contains the laws and ordinances which Bahá'u'lláh has revealed. Laws and ordinances are commandments which we have to obey. Laws are needed wherever people live in a community. Otherwise they do not know what they are allowed or not allowed to do. Without them, everything would soon get into a dreadful mess. You know, for example, that there are rules of the road. If everyone obeys the rules of the road, all goes well. But what a disaster it is if people do not. If we just drove through the traffic lights when they were red, or drove on the wrong side of the road or did not look properly when crossing the street, terrible accidents would happen.

Governments can make laws which the people of the land must obey. School governors and principals make rules which the students must obey. But the most profound laws for the re-organisation of life on this earth come to us from God. God, through His Messenger, sends into the world exactly those laws which are most needed to help mankind progress.

The laws revealed by a Messenger are quite different from the laws which people make for themselves. They have much more power, as do the words of a Messenger of God. The words of even the cleverest people in the world, or even of all the people together, can never have such a great influence as the words of God's Messengers.

Here is a clear example of this: Bahá'u'lláh revealed in the *Kitáb-i-Aqdas*: 'The Lord hath ordained that in every city a House of Justice be established . . .' This means that in every area a Local Spiritual Assembly, which will in the future be called a House of Justice, must be formed.

Now, over a hundred years later, there are more than 32,000 Local Spiritual Assemblies all over the world. Because of these words of Bahá'u'lláh, thousands of men and women have left their homes to go and live somewhere else, sometimes in countries which are very far from their native land. This has often meant a big effort and a lot of sacrifice but yet they managed it. They would do anything to carry out this commandment of Bahá'u'lláh.

At this time, in our own day, we cannot even imagine how great the influence of the *Kitáb-i-Aqdas* is going to be. The Most Holy Book will be distributed all over the world. People in every city and every village will read it and obey its laws.

People all over the world will be protected by the laws of the *Kitáb-i-Aqdas*. The world will become a safe world. Bahá'u'lláh Himself has said that His laws and ordin-

ances are 'the highest means for the maintenance of order in the world and the security of its peoples'.

All over the world schools will be established. A time will come when all children will learn to read and write. This has not happened yet; there are still millions of children who do not go to school or who spend much too little time at school. All over the world people will not only speak the language of their own country but also a world language. Then everyone in the world will be able to speak to everyone else and write letters to each other, even though they may live in different countries.

All over the world people will fast from sunrise to sunset during the month of fasting and the obligatory prayers will be said everywhere, because this is what Bahá'u'lláh has enjoined in the Most Holy Book.

Not all the laws in the Most Holy Book apply to us as yet. That is not yet possible. It is like the rising of the sun. It is slow, it takes some time before the sun becomes really hot. In the same way, the laws of Bahá'u'lláh are gradually being introduced.

We can hardly imagine it. There are now so few people who know that Bahá'u'lláh is God's Messenger for this Age. But the time will come when people all over the world will obey the laws of the *Kitáb-i-Aqdas* for love of God.

36

Enemies Become Friends

How would you like to live in a neighbourhood where everyone was nasty to you, where it looked as if you had done something wrong even though you had not, where you were taunted and shouted at every time you went out? Anyone would hate it.

Yet this is what happened to Bahá'u'lláh and His followers in 'Akká. When they arrived from Adrianople, the people stood along the side of the road and shouted at them. It was so terrible that it was frightening.

For years the inhabitants of 'Akká thought that Bahá'u'lláh and His followers were wicked people who wanted to destroy the religion of God, who had betrayed the Sultán and were wild characters who were better off in prison. They thought it best to keep away from them as much as they possibly could.

The guards in the prison thought the same thing. That is why they were so often nasty and cruel to the Bahá'ís. But whatever the guards did to them, the prisoners were never angry but remained friendly and polite. When the guards saw this, they could not go on being so nasty to them.

The same thing happened with the citizens of 'Akká. How can you go on thinking wicked things about people whom you never see doing anything wrong? Well, there was one time when they acted very wrongly. That was when a small group of Bahá'ís killed Siyyid Muḥammad and two of his helpers because they were making life so miserable for Bahá'u'lláh and the Bahá'ís. But after a while everyone in 'Akká realised that Bahá'u'lláh strongly disapproved of that deed and that it caused Him a lot of sorrow.

Shaykh Maḥmúd lived in 'Akká. He was a fanatical Muslim. When the Sulṭán's decree was read in the mosque, saying that Bahá'u'lláh was to be banished to 'Akká, Shaykh Maḥmúd was furious. He could hardly control himself. He wanted to see Bahá'u'lláh and tell Him what he thought of Him. He even intended to curse Bahá'u'lláh and insult Him.

He went to the prison and told the guards to take him to Bahá'u'lláh. The guards were not supposed to allow anyone in. They were meant to see that Bahá'u'lláh spoke to no one. But Shaykh Maḥmúd was an important man in 'Akká and so they could not refuse him.

They told him, however, that he could only see Bahá'u'lláh if Bahá'u'lláh Himself would agree to it. Shaykh Maḥmúd had to wait for a few minutes. After a while the answer came. Shaykh Maḥmúd could see Bahá'u'lláh, but first he must change his intention. In astonishment, he went away. How could Bahá'u'lláh know what he had been going to do?

Shaykh Maḥmúd tried a second time to see Bahá'u'lláh. This time he hid a weapon under his clothing with which he thought he could attack Bahá'u'lláh. Again the guards had to go and ask Bahá'u'lláh whether He would agree to see him. A few moments later the answer came: Shaykh Maḥmúd must throw away what he was carrying.

Once again, Shaykh Maḥmúd was astonished. He had secretly hidden a weapon under his clothing. He thought

that no one knew. And yet Bahá'u'lláh knew. How could
He? He wondered: who is this Man who knows other
people's secrets?

For the third time he went to the prison. But now
Shaykh Maḥmúd had become quite a different person.
Now he no longer came with evil intentions, and now he
was let in. In Bahá'u'lláh's room he threw himself at His
feet and said he wanted to become one of His followers.

One of the governors of 'Akká also became a friend of
the Faith. Who was the cause of this? The enemies of the
Faith!

The enemies wanted the governor to become an enemy

of the Faith too. Then he would help them to make life difficult for Bahá'u'lláh, they thought. They had made a plan. They gave the governor the Writings of Bahá'u'lláh and asked him to read them. They thought that he would get very angry. But what happened?

Just the opposite! Through reading Bahá'u'lláh's Writings the governor began to have a high respect for Him instead. After that he often went to visit 'Abdu'l-Bahá and when he got to 'Abdu'l-Bahá's house he used to take off his shoes. The people of 'Akká used to say that if he had difficult problems he would go to 'Abdu'l-Bahá to ask him how to solve them.

This governor was once also allowed to visit Bahá'u'lláh. He asked Bahá'u'lláh then if he could do anything for Him. He wanted to render Him some service. Bahá'u'lláh asked for nothing for Himself. He asked for something which would do good to all the inhabitants of 'Akká.

There was an aqueduct near 'Akká. An aqueduct is a kind of water main above the ground. It could carry lovely fresh drinking water to 'Akká. But this aqueduct had been broken for the last thirty years. When the governor asked Bahá'u'lláh if he could render Him a service, Bahá'u'lláh asked him to have the aqueduct repaired. The governor made sure that this was done as quickly as possible.

Other things in 'Akká had changed. 'Akká had been a dry city for thousands of years, with a rainfall of only two inches a year. Only plants and trees which needed very little water could grow there. After Bahá'u'lláh had come to 'Akká gradually more rain began to fall. By the time He had been living in 'Akká for twenty years, it had a rainfall of thirty inches a year.

'Akká became quite a different place. There were wells

which had always contained brackish water which was undrinkable. Suddenly clear, fresh drinking water came out of them. When Bahá'u'lláh arrived in 'Akká it was a city where there was always a bad smell. The people even said that if a bird flew over it, it would fall to the ground from the stench. That is how bad it was! Gradually the air above 'Akká became clear and fresh too. 'Akká became a healthy place to live in, so healthy that there are now hospitals there for people who need good fresh air.

How did this change come about? The people of 'Akká knew how. They said it was because Bahá'u'lláh was living in their midst.

When Bahá'u'lláh and the Bahá'ís arrived in 'Akká the people thought they were criminals who ought to be in prison. Years later, they knew differently. The Bahá'ís were kind and honest people. A lot of things had changed in 'Akká through the coming of Bahá'u'lláh.

Now the people had a much better understanding of Who Bahá'u'lláh was. When they spoke of Him now, they did so with the greatest respect.

37

Mazra'ih

Bahá'u'lláh had been living as a prisoner in 'Akká for nine years. All this time He had never once been out of the city. According to the decree of Sultán 'Abdu'l-'Azíz, Bahá'u'lláh should not leave the house where He was imprisoned.

At first this decree was strictly carried out. Bahá'u'lláh was allowed no visitors. He was not even allowed to speak to the followers who had come with Him to the same prison. Only His wife and children were allowed to see Him. Later, the gates of the prison were opened, and pilgrims were permitted to come into the presence of Bahá'u'lláh.

When Bahá'u'lláh lived some years later in the House of 'Abbúd He had no freedom either. He was always indoors. His only exercise was walking up and down in His room.

Then one day He said: 'I have not gazed on verdure for nine years. The country is the world of the soul, the city is the world of bodies.'

'Abdu'l-Bahá knew well what these words meant: Bahá'u'lláh was longing for the country. 'Abdu'l-Bahá immediately went in search of a country house.

He found one in Mazra'ih, three kilometres from 'Akká. It was a lovely villa in beautiful surroundings with a stream running by. It belonged to Muḥammad Páshá

Ṣafwat. But he did not live there; he preferred to live in his house in ‘Akká. There he was nearer to his friends and could enjoy their company. He himself was an invalid and so could not get about very easily. He felt too cut off in his villa at Mazra‘ih.

‘Abdu’l-Bahá went to see him and asked if he would rent his villa. This amazed Muḥammad Páshá Ṣafwat. He had never expected the Bahá’ís to ask him such a thing. He was really an enemy of the Faith and had often tried to oppose it. Now here was 'Abdu'l-Bahá coming to ask if he could rent his villa. Eventually he agreed and let 'Abdu'l-Bahá have it for a low rent. 'Abdu'l-Bahá immediately paid enough rent for five years and sent workmen to put the house and garden in order.

But there was another problem. Bahá'u'lláh was not allowed out of the city. The Sultán's strict decree was still in force; not one letter of it had changed. It was true that the Bahá'ís now had more freedom, they could have visitors and could visit others. But could they leave the city?

'Abdu'l-Bahá decided to put it to the test. One day he wanted to go to Mazra'ih to have a look at the villa for himself. What would happen if he were to walk out through the gate of 'Akká? Would the soldiers standing on guard there stop him and send him back? Or would they let him through without saying anything?

'Abdu'l-Bahá walked calmly out through the gate. He acted as if this was an everyday occurrence. Luckily, nothing happened! The soldiers just let him through. Next day, he went again, with some friends and officials, and once more the soldiers allowed him to pass. Not long afterwards 'Abdu'l-Bahá held a large feast outside the city and invited the authorities and officials of 'Akká to it. Once again there was no problem. It was as if the Sultán's decree no longer existed.

Then 'Abdu'l-Bahá went to Bahá'u'lláh and said: 'The palace at Mazra'ih is ready for You, and a carriage to drive You there.'

But Bahá'u'lláh would not go. He said: 'I am a prisoner.'

'Abdu'l-Bahá tried a second and even a third time. But Bahá'u'lláh still said 'No'. 'Abdu'l-Bahá did not dare to insist.

He went to see the Muftí of 'Akká, who was the leader of the Muslims.

This man was devoted to Bahá'u'lláh. 'Abdu'l-Bahá told the Muftí what had happened and asked if he would help. He said to the Muftí: 'You are daring. Go tonight to His Holy Presence, fall on your knees before Him, take hold of His hands and do not let go until He promises to leave the city.'

The Muftí went at once to Bahá'u'lláh, went down on his knees, took His hands in his own, kissed them and asked: 'Why do you not leave the city?'

Bahá'u'lláh then gave the same answer as He had given to 'Abdu'l-Bahá: 'I am a prisoner.'

The Muftí replied: 'God forbid! Who has the power to make you a prisoner? You have kept Yourself in prison. It was your own will to be imprisoned, and now I beg you to come out and go to the palace. It is beautiful and verdant. The trees are lovely, and the oranges like balls of fire!'

Each time that Bahá'u'lláh said He was a prisoner and could not go, the Muftí took His hands and kissed them. Again and again he begged Bahá'u'lláh to leave the city. Again and again Bahá'u'lláh refused because He was a prisoner. But the Muftí kept it up for a whole hour. At last Bahá'u'lláh said:

'Very good.'

Next day the carriage stood ready to bring Bahá'u'lláh to Mazra'ih. Officially, Bahá'u'lláh was still a prisoner Who was not allowed to leave 'Akká. But the carriage drove through the gates of the city without anyone saying a word.

There was now no one who troubled to see that the strict decree of the powerful Sulṭán 'Abdu'l-'Azíz was carried out.

144

38

More Freedom

A lot had changed since Bahá'u'lláh had arrived in 'Akká from Adrianople. He now lived in a lovely country villa at Mazra'ih, in the heart of nature, of which He was so fond. Two years later He moved to a larger house. This was the Mansion of Bahjí. 'Abdu'l-Bahá had also arranged this; he had rented it for his Father.

Now Bahá'u'lláh had much more freedom. He and His family could go out to the countryside to camp. He often went to a beautiful garden on a small island in a river which was near 'Akká. Bahá'u'lláh would go there with His family and followers for a picnic. He sometimes stayed there for several weeks. He slept in a little garden house there. It was such a lovely spot that it was given the name of Riḍván Garden, after the Garden of Riḍván near Baghdád where Bahá'u'lláh had announced that He was God's Messenger for this Age.

'Abdu'l-Bahá was very happy when he saw his Father sitting on a seat in the garden, in the shadow of a tree, with so many lovely flowers and shrubs around Him. That was much better than the grey walls of 'Akká which Bahá'u'lláh had had to look at for years.

'Abdu'l-Bahá did not go to live with Bahá'u'lláh outside the city. He stayed in 'Akká. He did this in order to serve and protect the Faith as much as possible. If someone had to speak to the authorities, 'Abdu'l-Bahá

did this. If there were difficulties, 'Abdu'l-Bahá would solve them. 'Abdu'l-Bahá was a shield that protected Bahá'u'lláh and the believers from trouble.

And there was trouble often enough. There were still people who wished to oppose the Faith.

One of these was 'Abdu'r-Rahmán. He was governor of 'Akká at the time when Bahá'u'lláh lived there. 'Abdu'r-Rahmán was always friendly towards the Bahá'ís. If he met 'Abdu'l-Bahá, he was very polite. But on the other hand, he often had secret talks with the opponents of the Faith and together they made plans to frustrate Bahá'u'lláh. They wrote reports to important members of the government. In these they reminded them of Sultán 'Abdu'l-'Azíz's decree that Bahá'u'lláh and His followers were not allowed to speak to the people of 'Akká. But, said these reports, the Bahá'ís can go and come where they please. They even have shops in 'Akká where they make a good living. And they can talk to anyone they like.

After they had written a great many such reports, an order came from the government: the Bahá'ís must close their shops.

'Abdu'r-Rahmán and his friends were delighted. They had got their way and they were going to see that the order was carried out. They wanted to do so in such a way that everyone in the city could see what was happening. What a bad reputation the Bahá'ís would get when everyone could see that the governor had ordered them to shut their shops. This was exactly what 'Abdu'r-

Raḥmán and his helpers wanted.

On the morning agreed, 'Abdu'r-Raḥmán and his helpers walked through the city. They were going to tell all the Bahá'ís that they could no longer keep shops. They got to the first shop. It was closed. And the second, it was closed too. They went to all the Bahá'ís' shops. They were all closed!

How had this happened? Bahá'u'lláh knew what 'Abdu'r-Raḥmán was planning and He had told the Bahá'ís to keep their shops closed that day.

'Abdu'r-Raḥmán said: 'They don't open their shops very early but it won't be long before they are here.'

'Abdu'r-Raḥmán and his helpers waited for two hours. And still no Bahá'í turned up to open his shop.

Then came the Muftí of 'Akká. He was the leader of the Muslims in the city. You could tell by his face that something was wrong. He had a telegram in his hand. It was from 'Abdu'r-Raḥmán's superior. It said that 'Abdu'r-Raḥmán had been dismissed.

Now 'Abdu'r-Raḥmán was no longer governor and could no longer forbid the Bahá'ís to keep shops in 'Akká!

Everyone was astonished. How had this happened? How could 'Abdu'r-Raḥmán be dismissed just when everyone thought the Bahá'ís were going to be badly humiliated?

Someone asked 'Abdu'l-Bahá if he had complained to 'Abdu'r-Raḥmán's superiors about him. 'Abdu'l-Bahá replied that he had not. But he did say that he had said a great many prayers.

This took place when Bahá'u'lláh still lived in 'Akká. But even afterwards, when He lived at Mazra'ih and Bahjí, the opponents did many irritating things. But they could not make Bahá'u'lláh's life as difficult as it had been before. They could not change the fact that Bahá'u'lláh lived in a beautiful house outside 'Akká, even though the Sulṭán's decree was still in force.

39

Mount Carmel

The opponents of the new Faith thought that they could destroy it. That is why they had banished Bahá'u'lláh to 'Akká. They thought they would hear no more of Bahá'u'lláh and that the new Faith would soon die out.

Is that possible? If God sends a new Messenger to the world, is it possible for ordinary people to hold back His work, which is the work of God?

Of course not. People cannot frustrate the Plan of God.

Bahá'u'lláh's opponents had certainly tried. But what happened? Instead of holding back the Plan of God they assisted it. They made sure that Bahá'u'lláh would be banished to 'Akká. In this way Bahá'u'lláh went to the Holy Land, which was exactly what God had planned and the Prophets had foretold.

Mount Carmel is a holy mountain. It can be seen across the bay from 'Akká. It is known as the Mountain of God. Thousands of years previously the prophets of Israel had prophesied about this mountain. One of them, the Prophet Isaiah, foretold that Carmel would 'behold the Glory of the Lord'. The 'Glory of the Lord,' to Whom might this refer? Just think for a moment what the name 'Bahá'u'lláh' means. The time had now come for Carmel to 'behold' the 'Glory' of her Lord.

Sultán 'Abdu'l-'Azíz's decree that Bahá'u'lláh was to speak to no one was still in force. But now Bahá'u'lláh could go wherever He wished and speak to whom He wished. The opponents of the Faith could not prevent it. They could not prevent Bahá'u'lláh going to Mount Carmel and pitching His tent upon it. He did so four times.

One day Bahá'u'lláh stood with 'Abdu'l-Bahá on the slopes of the mountain. He then pointed to an expanse of rock in front of Him. Bahá'u'lláh told 'Abdu'l-Bahá that the Shrine which was to hold the remains of the Báb must be built here.

It was now forty years since the Báb had been executed in Tabríz. His body had afterwards been thrown somewhere outside the city. The second night after His death some of the Bábís had fetched the Báb's body and hidden it. From then onwards it was kept hidden in Persia, so well hidden that the enemies of the Faith had never been able to find it.

'Abdu'l-Bahá could not start to build the Shrine of the Báb immediately. After the passing of Bahá'u'lláh, the Covenant-breakers tried to stop Him from doing so. Yet 'Abdu'l-Bahá continued to carry out his Father's instructions. It took nineteen long years to complete a simple structure. Then the body of the Báb could be buried in the spot where Bahá'u'lláh had indicated.

At first the Shrine looked very simple. Forty years later, Shoghi Effendi, the Guardian of the Faith, had a beautiful superstructure and dome built over it, and created lovely gardens all around it. He called the Shrine of the Báb the Queen of Carmel.

A few days after Bahá'u'lláh had shown 'Abdu'l-Bahá the place for the Shrine, Bahá'u'lláh revealed the Tablet of Carmel. This took place at the top of the mountain, on a promontory. In the future a splendid Temple will be built at that spot.

The Tablet of Carmel is a very special Tablet. In it Bahá'u'lláh says that God will soon sail His Ark on Carmel. God's 'Ark' is the Universal House of Justice which has been established upon Mount Carmel. This too is in fulfilment of the Plan of God.

In the future Mount Carmel will be the centre of the world. People will come from all parts of the world to visit it. The Seat of the Universal House of Justice which now stands upon Mount Carmel will be joined by other buildings belonging to the World Centre of the Bahá'í Faith. They will be built in an arc on the mountainside, with beautiful gardens around them.

When the World Centre buildings are finished, a wonderful time for mankind will begin: the Lesser Peace. Then there will be no more war anywhere in the world. It will not be long now – it will happen before the year 2000! 'Abdu'l-Bahá has foretold this.

40

The Ascension of Bahá'u'lláh

'I am well pleased with you all. Ye have rendered many services, and been very assiduous in your labours. Ye have come here every morning and every evening. May God assist you to remain united. May He aid you to exalt the Cause of the Lord of being.'

These were the words of Bahá'u'lláh to the followers who were in His household. He spoke kindly to them, as He always did. And yet they were sad, very sad indeed.

Bahá'u'lláh was ill. He had been ill before. But this time His followers were dreadfully anxious. He was sinking all the time. If this continued, it would not be long before Bahá'u'lláh was no longer with them. What were they to do? How could they live without Him?

Two of the followers, Mírzá 'Andalíb and Mírzá Baṣṣár, were also very sad. Weeping, they kept returning to Bahá'u'lláh's bedside. They begged Him to let them die in His place. They wanted to save the life of Bahá'u'lláh for the world, even if only for a short time.

But Bahá'u'lláh did not get better. For three weeks He was ill and then He passed away on 29 May 1892. He was then 74 years old.

'The Sun of Bahá has set.' This is how the telegram began which 'Abdu'l-Bahá sent to the Sulṭán immediately after the Ascension of Bahá'u'lláh. In this telegram he informed the Sulṭán that the body of Bahá'u'lláh would

be buried in a small building just beside the mansion at Bahjí. The Sulṭán gave his permission. Bahá'u'lláh was buried that same day in the evening just after sunset.

The sorrow of the Bahá'ís was great. But the people of 'Akká also deeply regretted that Bahá'u'lláh had died. Most of them really did not understand Who Bahá'u'lláh was. They did not know that He, like Muḥammad, was a Messenger of God. But they did realise that a very special Person had died. Many people from the city and the nearby villages went to Bahjí to the house in which Bahá'u'lláh had lived and where He was buried. They stayed there for a whole week, inconsolable.

How things had changed! Do you remember what the people of 'Akká did when Bahá'u'lláh arrived there first? They stood along the side of the street to mock at Him and His followers and to curse them. Now, twenty-five years later, they were weeping with sorrow that He had left them.

For the last forty years of His life on earth, Bahá'u'lláh was really a prisoner all the time. His imprisonment began in Ṭihrán, in the Síyáh-Chál, a dark and filthy dungeon under the ground. A few days after He was released the news came that He must leave the country. He then went with His family to Baghdád. There, Mírzá Yaḥyá made His life so difficult that He departed for Sulaymáníyyih. For a long time He lived there, high in the mountains, all alone. The family of Bahá'u'lláh did not know where He was.

When He returned to Baghdád, the followers of the Báb had almost lost their faith. Bahá'u'lláh gave them new courage. Because of Him, the Faith began to grow again. So many people came to Baghdád to see Him that the opponents became jealous and made sure that He would have to leave Baghdád. He then went to Constantinople and from there to Adrianople. In Adrianople, Mírzá Yaḥyá did many wicked things because he himself wanted to be leader. He told all kinds of lies about Bahá'u'lláh until the Sulṭán decided to banish Bahá'u'lláh to the prison in 'Akká. After nine years, He left the city of 'Akká and was able to live in a country house. Until the time of His death He remained a prisoner of the state.

It seemed as if the work of the opponents of the Faith had been to make sure that Bahá'u'lláh was banished from one place to another. But this was not so. For each new banishment fitted into the Plan of God. It was the Plan of God which brought Bahá'u'lláh to the Holy Land.

Bahá'u'lláh sailed across the Black Sea when He went to Constantinople and across the Mediterranean Sea

155

when He was sent to 'Akká. He lived in the mountains of Sulaymáníyyih and He ascended Mount Carmel.

That was the Plan of God. Almost three thousand years before, the Prophet Micah had foretold: 'He shall come from sea to sea and from mountain to mountain.'

41

'Abdu'l-Bahá

Who was going to lead the Bahá'ís now? Bahá'u'lláh was no longer on this earth. They could no longer ask Him for advice. The sorrow of the friends knew no bounds.

The enemies of the Faith, on the contrary, were glad. So were the Sulṭán in Constantinople and the Sháh of Persia. They were delighted. The Bahá'ís they had been persecuting now had no Leader. Once again they thought that the new Faith would soon die out.

Was this true? Would God let this happen? It had never happened and was not going to happen now.

During His life, Bahá'u'lláh had written His Will and Testament. In this He told His family and followers what they must do after His passing. The Will and Testament was sealed with Bahá'u'lláh's seal. This was very important. No one could secretly open the Will to read it or change anything in it. Bahá'u'lláh had given the Will to 'Abdu'l-Bahá to keep safely.

On the ninth day after the Ascension of Bahá'u'lláh the Will was read. First, 'Abdu'l-Bahá had called nine Bahá'ís together. Then the seal was broken and the Will opened. They could all see that it had never been opened before that moment. Then it was read.

No mistake was possible. The Will revealed clearly that Bahá'u'lláh had appointed 'Abdu'l-Bahá to be His successor. 'Abdu'l-Bahá was now the leader of the Faith.

Everyone must obey 'Abdu'l-Bahá. If they obeyed him, they would be obeying God. If they did not obey him, they would be disobeying God. If they read something in the Writings of Bahá'u'lláh which they could not understand, they were to ask 'Abdu'l-Bahá to explain it. Only 'Abdu'l-Bahá could explain the words of Bahá'u'lláh correctly. No one else could do so.

For thirty years, 'Abdu'l-Bahá led the Faith. Each day he worked from early in the morning to late at night to spread it and protect it. He wrote thousands of letters. More and more people came to see him, people from very different countries and of various religions. In the house of 'Abdu'l-Bahá it was as if such differences did not exist. In 'Abdu'l-Bahá's home there was unity among all people.

Unity among all peoples: it was for this that God gave Bahá'u'lláh to the world. That is the reason Bahá'u'lláh established a new religion. The Faith is like a tiny seed. From that tiny seed comes first of all a very small plant. That little plant gets bigger and grows until it becomes a mighty tree. When it is still small we cannot imagine that later on it will be a big, strong tree.

It is just the same with the Bahá'í Faith. There are millions of people who have never heard of it. It is still like a very young plant which you can hardly see. It will become so strong and mighty that it will shelter all the people on the earth.